Fire Within

Jesse
the
Mexican
Superhero

Fire Within

31 life lessons on evangelism, discipleship and the gospel

JESSE EISENHOUR

Published by

www.nebthos.com

This book is dedicated to my wife.

First, because it was her idea in the first place. Second, because what you don't get to read in this book are the stories of what is happening at home. Without her, this book would not have been written. Without her, there would be no stories. Her support means the world to me.

(I considered doing the "spiritual thing" and dedicating it to Jesus, but the entire thing is about Him, so I wanted to bless my wife, who is rarely mentioned.)

TABLE OF CONTENTS

AUTHOR'S WIFE'S NOTE

Don't skip the Author's Note.

AUTHOR'S NOTE

In order for you to understand some of these stories, you're going to have to understand a little about Time to Revive, the tools we have, and the framework that we use to share the gospel.

Time to Revive (TTR or Revive, for short) is a ministry based out of Richardson, Texas. Our mission is "equipping the saints to share the gospel and make disciples." Our goal is not just to lead people to Jesus, but to get them to a point where they are whole-heartedly following Christ through discipleship, which we offer to everyone that gives their life to the Lord.

When we go to a city, we look for hunger, humility, and unity. We do our best to network with churches of different denominations. We only ask that they focus on what unites us instead of the minor things that cause division. It is often said at TTR that if you believe in the death, burial, and resurrection of Jesus then we are willing to work with you. It doesn't mean we will ignore the things that are out of alignment, as much as it does mean that we're willing to trust that the Holy Spirit will do His job. We have team members all across the USA, who have left their careers to do this full and part time. Many of us had never been in full-time ministry before working for Revive. Each outreach is labeled after whatever state we're in. So in Indiana it's called "reviveINDIANA."

I came into contact with Revive when they first came to Indiana back in January 2015. My life was radically turned upside down as I watched what the Lord did. Whites, Hispanics, and Blacks came together under the banner of Christ. Methodists, Baptists, A/G, Mennonites, Amish, and non-denominational churches were all represented. Ethnicity didn't seem to matter. Theology wasn't discussed in an argumentative way, but in a genuine attempt to understand each other's perspective as we grew to love each other.

I have been with the ministry first as a volunteer and now as a team member for three years and have been to more cities than I can remember, all to help pass on the training that changed my life.

At Time to Revive we have an amazing process that allows for employees, volunteers, and trainees from the city to split up quickly and randomly so that you're not on a team with someone you know. (You can be, but the point is to teach new people how to share the gospel and make disciples, not to hang out with our friends.) When a story talks about a team member, it is most likely referring to someone I met that day (or week) and I am teaching them how to do this as a lifestyle (though there are times when we do team up with other TTR employees). Each team is made up of four people and that team will discuss where to go and who to "encounter." An encounter is the term we use to describe when we interact with someone with the intention to share the gospel.

Before you go out on a team, you get a bag with the physical tools that we use: four Bibles (three in English and one in Spanish), wristbands, and gospel cards (which have the same verses on it that you can use instead of the Bible). While you're out, we encourage you to wear a wristband and keep some in your pocket so that they are easily accessible when you meet someone and to keep the Bible in a hidden place, like a pocket or a purse. I like to tell people (who aren't pacifists [if you are, ignore this part... I love you!]) to carry the Bible like a gun. Keep it handy, but people will be more at ease if they don't know you have it.

We always leave everything up to the Holy Spirit's guidance as we go through each encounter. Some things may vary, but ultimately what won't change are the verses we use with the Bible and wristband. On the band there are five colors: yellow, black, red, blue, and green that match the Bible. The Bible has an extra color, orange, which I refer to lovingly as the "bonus fry." (You know...like when you thought you ate all the fries, but you look into the bag, and whoop! There's another fry! BONUS FRY!)

We usually ask someone how we can pray for them first, but regardless of whether or not you do that first or last, at some point you're going to want to give them the wristband. Most people love it because it's free. I usually say something along the lines of, "Each color on the band has a word to go with it, would you be interested in knowing what those colors represent?" I try really hard to be sensitive to my surroundings and ask if they have some time to go through it. When we're ready, we hand THEM the Bible and let them know we'll be starting with the color yellow. There are tabs on the Bible, and the tabs are numbered.

We have them open to tab number one and read the passage that is already highlighted. The verse is Romans 3:23, "For all have sinned and fall short of the glory of God" (NASB). We ask what that means to them, or if they know what the word "sin" means. Either way, they need to recognize that we all have sinned. I usually say something like, "It means nobody's perfect," or "We all jack up our lives." If they agree and believe that, we tell them that the color yellow on the band represents sin.

Then we move to number two, the black tab, and have them read the verse. This one is Romans 6:23, "For the wages of sin is death, but the free gift of God is eternal life in Christ Jesus our Lord" (NASB). The word you want to emphasize here is "wages." You want them to understand that the "wages of sin," or what we earn for our sin, is death. The verse does go on to talk about the free gift, but because we talk about that later, I don't usually bring that part up, UNLESS the person is really bummed already, and sort of acting like they don't want to continue because the news sucks so far.

I will ask if they believe that everyone dies, because according to Genesis, death entered the world specifically because of our sin. It is both physical and spiritual. I try to make sure they understand that the verse is talking about eternal death, which is referred to as hell. So the color black represents death.

(FYI since this book is about my stories, I figured you should know that my favorite color is black...not because of this verse... just because it looks so nice. My hair is naturally black because I am half-Mexican, and it's nice to just wear things that match your hair.)

Let's move on to number three. This red verse is Romans 5:8. "But God demonstrates His own love toward us, in that while we were yet sinners, Christ died for us" (NASB). The focus word is "demonstrate." We usually try to have fun with it and ask for volunteers to demonstrate something. One time I had a push-up contest between a studly young football player and a pastor who used to do competitive weightlifting. Anything to make it fun and alive!

Next I like to focus on "while we were yet sinners" because it is referring to the fact that you don't have to get your life together before you come to Jesus. We point out the fact that first you come to Jesus, and then He will clean you up. That's called sanctification. The red verse stands for love. If we want it, it can wipe away the sin and death, and the way we do that is through the next two.

Number four is the color blue (even though it looks purple on the Bible…the printers made it wrong… It's all good). Either before or after they read it I say, "If you were standing at the gates of heaven and they asked, 'Why should we let you in?' what would you say?" If they are "works based" (they think their works will save them), it will come out here. If they know it's because they've been born again, and they're living out a real relationship with Jesus, that will come out as well. This verse is Ephesians 2:8-9. "For by grace you have been saved through faith; and that not of yourselves, it is the gift of God; not as a result of works, so that no one may boast" (NASB).

The fifth and final verse is the color green. "If you confess with your mouth Jesus as Lord, and believe in your heart that God raised Him from the dead, you will be saved; for with the heart a person believes, resulting in righteousness, and with the mouth he confesses, resulting in salvation" (Rom. 10:9-10 NASB). Because this verse is really wordy, sometimes people understand it, but they usually don't. I try to help them understand the words "confess" and "Lord" because they aren't super common. Most people think the word "confess" means you have to sit in a booth and tell a priest everything you've done wrong. That isn't what it means. We aren't telling people that it's wrong to do that, because it is absolutely good to confess your sins to one another. However, this just means "to admit."

When I explain "Lord," I ask if they've heard of a landlord. (I learned that from a friend!) We just want them to understand that you're giving lordship over your own life to Jesus. HE is now in charge of the way you spend money, the way you talk to your spouse, and everything else you do goes through Him. It also says you have to believe in your heart God raised him from the dead. We have to be willing to admit that Jesus died on a cross, was raised to life, and then rode a cloud into heaven like an elevator, and never re-died.

This is when I direct them to the back cover of the Bible. It has a question on it. "Is there anything or anyone that would keep you from accepting the free gift of life in Jesus today?" It's a super non-threatening way to ask people if they want Jesus to be in charge of their life and to save them from their sin. If they say yes, that something is in the way, we help them remove it. If they say no, we ask them if they would like to do that now, with us.

We give them three options. The back of the Bible has a sinner's prayer on it that they can use if they'd like, they could repeat after you, or they could pray on their own. My favorite is for them to pray on their own, but it's more common to want to repeat after someone.

That's when I go through the orange tab/bonus fry. It talks about the Holy Spirit dwelling inside them and how they are a "new creation." It also has tangible next steps: getting them plugged into community or discipleship, baptism, reading the Bible, prayer, and sharing their faith. Lots of people want discipleship and sometimes people want a church. You'd be surprised to see how many people would get baptized if you asked them.

What is super fun is that our ministry has a massive box truck that was converted to be used for mobile baptisms. It had been previously used for advertising in Dallas and was donated to TTR. It has clear sides so that you can see straight through it and the scriptures printed on the bottom of both sides of the truck. Inside there is a lidded horse trough that we fill with water, along with bins filled with every size of clothes, and towels. It even has a hamper! The baptism truck allows us to baptize anyone, anytime, anywhere!

If our host church doesn't have a baptismal, we can live-stream from the truck into the sanctuary so people don't have to go outside to watch the baptism. When we are out on the street and someone gets baptized we try to stream that as well. We stream as much as possible. During the normal outreach, every morning and evening service are live-streamed, both on the website and on Facebook Live.

I hope this note will provide context for many of the stories to follow, and if it was overwhelming...don't worry, there's a cheat sheet in the back of the book for quick reference of the colors and verses.

INTRODUCTION

The intention of this book is to inspire, motivate, and equip you to share the gospel and make disciples. All of the stories you are about to read are true, but written from my perspective. I readily admit that I've not always made the right decisions or had the right motivation, but I am certainly on a journey. Most of you have way more to offer the lost than I do, and I again admit that I have a lot of learning to do, but my hope is that this will create a hunger inside of you to do something with what you've been given. My drive for the gospel comes from deep within. Like the prophet Jeremiah said,

> But if I say I'll never mention the Lord
> or speak in His name,
> His word burns in my heart like a fire.
> It's like a fire in my bones!
> I am worn out trying to hold it in!
> I can't do it! (Jer. 20:9)

This is how I feel. My life has been wrecked by Jesus and it'll never look the same. I have seen things most people only read about in books because I have chosen to step out in faith and follow Jesus. There is no turning back for me. I'm in.

My hope is that these stories will challenge you to say something to that guy over there that has passed you, now several times. My hope is that this book will help you to know it's normal to be afraid, but the righteous are "as bold as lions" (Prov. 28:1). The funny thing about lions is this, I don't believe lions cower while hunting. I think that they believe they are the most dangerous thing around.

This is the way it should be for us, but since most of us are still immature in our faith we forget that the God that spoke the universe into being lives inside us. I'm here to gently…but firmly…nudge you and myself along. (Haha.)

DAY 1
MIDDLEBURY, IN

A FRESH START

For your information, I have never been in a fight. In fact, I have the kind of personality that would require me to run, as fast as possible, away from whatever person would want to beat the daylights out of me. The closest I have ever been to fighting was in middle school during gym class...when I had to wrestle a guy. I enjoy a good verbal confrontation, but I tend to back down when I know someone is getting angry. I didn't know that on this day I would be breaking up a fight.

The Lord put it on our hearts to go to a specific trailer park. As we pulled in, there were two ladies sitting in front of a trailer and I immediately felt the need to talk to them. Two of us went over to see what opportunities the Lord would present.

We were sharing the gospel with their family when all of a sudden the trailer next to us sounded as if it was going to explode. Shouting, slamming, and sounds as if someone tried to throw someone else through a wall were coming from inside.

A young man came out of another house, dialing 911. He told everyone outside to go inside their homes, because "he" was out of control. It wasn't safe, so he was calling the police.

The family we had been sharing the gospel with decided to take their kids and head inside the house. I asked if I should go over there and see how I could help, and everyone told me no, to stay out of it and get to a safe place. Something inside me kept telling me to get closer. My mind was racing with questions, but for some strange reason there was no fear.

At that time, there was a woman who came out of the house, power walking away from it, and after every so many steps would turn around to scream at someone in the house. Then a young man came running out of the house, screaming profanity at the lady and following her. By this time I was right in front of the house, and I could see everything.

Something (I think it was the Holy Spirit) compelled me to do something. But what?

Another man, who was much older, came out of the house yelling at the young man to calm down and that he shouldn't behave that way. The young man turned and ran up to him putting his finger in his face, while screaming at him, and then turning back to scream at the woman, his mom, who was by now pretty much out of sight.

The older man, who turned out to be his stepdad, kept yelling at the young man, causing him to pick up a rock in front of me and chuck it at his stepdad, barely missing and denting his house. At this point, I couldn't just watch.

I started to talk to the young man, asking what his name was and what was going on. He turned to me and started to yell at me, telling me about how he was tired of his stepdad and mom fighting all the time. He used much more colorful language to describe them and how they are always fighting. He said he just wanted peace.

I firmly spoke to him, "You said you want peace, do you want it now?" He nodded. I grabbed his hand and I could feel the blood in his veins pulsating like crazy, and I firmly prayed, "Peace, in Jesus' name."

Immediately I felt the young man's pulse slow down to normal. Then I started asking him again about who he was and what all had happened. He told me his name and began to calmly explain the situation.

While he was talking, the Lord put a picture of a circle in my mind, so I asked him, "Do you feel like you are trapped in a circle, where you think things are going to get better and they never pan out, and in fact they often get worse, causing all hope to be non-existent?"

He said, "Yes, absolutely."

I felt compelled to ask, "Do you want out of the circle?"

He said yes, that all he wanted was a fresh start. I told him that I could give that to him if he would be willing to listen and do some things he may not want to do. He agreed.

I first felt the need to have him pray to forgive his mom. To be honest it was the last thing I wanted to say to this guy, but it just came out of me. He understood right away that it was necessary and he bowed his head and repeated a prayer after me, but the coolest part was that he started to pray on his own. He began to apologize to the Lord for his side of the mess, acknowledging that he was also to blame. On his own, this non-Christian man began to repent before the Lord, wiping the tears from his eyes as he prayed.

I told him that I was proud of him. It is hard to forgive people, especially when things are fresh, and you'd rather beat them than forgive them. I gave him a wristband and said, "Now, this is next."

I told him that he already began in his prayer with the yellow color on our wristband, because he was starting to acknowledge his own sins. I was able to explain three of the colors when the police showed up. At that point I was pretty sure everything was over. I prayed that the Lord would allow me to finish sharing the gospel, but it sounded like the cops were going to take him.

Finally they finished and decided to allow him to stay. Now his mom, brother, and stepdad were all standing there with us. We began to explain the rest of the gospel, even as the stepdad went inside the house. Before we asked if he'd like to be saved, I let his mom know what all we had talked about prior to her coming over with the officer. I explained that he was sorry and that he was ready to get out of the crazy cycle.

She was thrilled that we were sharing Christ with her son. So, I finally asked if he was ready for his new beginning. He said YES. So I led him through a prayer of salvation!

As we prayed, another teammate walked up. When we were done praying, my teammate and I told him about how he's a new creation, now the old things have passed away and the new things have come. I even went through and explained the fruit of the Spirit, so that he would know that everything he had been lacking before to control his anger now lived inside of him and the fruit would begin to manifest.

We explained that he would now find himself wanting to live differently. We also explained we weren't about to have him go it alone, but that we wanted to surround him with another man who would be willing to walk out this journey with him. He agreed to let my teammate disciple him!

2 Corinthians 5:17 says, "This means that anyone who belongs to Christ has become a new person. The old life is gone; a new life has begun!"

"I just need a fresh start" is one of the most common things I have heard from the people I encounter on the street. People's lives, even though they may look perfect on the outside, may be in utter turmoil behind closed doors. As a society we have found so many ways to mask our pain, feeling as if we are obligated to never have a bad day. All that I have ever asked of anyone is that they tell the truth when I am on the street. You tell me the truth, and I will tell you the truth. My feelings never get hurt from an honest response. But I hate it when I feel like someone has lied to my face.

We have all had bad days. We have all had days when we have said something we wished we wouldn't, or done something we wished we could take back. We are all at different places in our sanctification process and need to recognize the grace necessary for each of us to grow.

> The faithful love of the Lord never ends!
>   His mercies never cease.
> Great is His faithfulness;
>   His mercies begin afresh each morning. (Lam. 3:22-23)

The young man we encountered that day just wanted a fresh start. Maybe as you read this, you know that you recently messed up.

You too are living in a cycle you wish you could get out of. The good news for you (assuming you are already saved) is that you get a fresh new start every day. The mercies of the Lord begin all over again for you. Not to give you license to go do whatever evil thing you can imagine, but to release you from the burden of having to perform and "be good." Just go, live for Jesus, be empowered by His love and compassion, and take your fresh start.

Today through the power of the Holy Spirit, you can show grace to the coworker who nags you all day long. Today you can overcome the urge to overreact. Today you can speak kindly to your wife. Today you can ask someone for forgiveness.

Today you have your fresh start.

RESPONSE

Now is the time you have to make a decision. Am I going to respond to what I just read, or will I let it pass me by? There are blank pages in between each chapter because we are anticipating that you will respond accordingly. Journal your own testimonies/journey here.

DAY 2
BEMIDJI, MN

SOMETIMES YOU FEEL LIKE A CIRCUS

Do you do things that naturally draw attention to yourself? Or do you prefer to remain incognito? At an outreach in Bemidji, my seven-year-old son Josiah wanted to come out with me because he heard that I would be driving the baptism truck. When you're in this truck, it's so big that you have no choice but to be seen by all. Often times, people will pass you trying to take a picture. It always makes us feel like a circus while we're driving it around, but it also seems to scream that we believe people are going to be saved. We show up expecting results.

There was a team that we were supposed to meet up with, but there was a mix-up and we never actually ended in the same place. That morning the Lord put it on my heart to go to a particular part of town. Because we arrived in the morning, not a lot of people were out. I slowly, and conspicuously, drove through the neighborhood and asked the Lord where I should turn. We wove around and eventually came to an area where there were kids playing in the streets.

As we came closer to them, I had to slow down so I wouldn't run them over. There was a lady watching the kids from a lawn chair outside her apartment and smoking. I rolled my window down and asked if they had ever seen a truck like this. She stood up and said no, with a big smile. Josiah and I got out and began asking how we could pray.

All of a sudden people started coming out of the woodwork. There were about fifteen people outside looking at the baptism truck all at once, and a few of them let us pray. Josiah and I gave each of them a wristband, which brought even more people out. Everyone wants a wristband, right? I asked if anyone wanted to know what the colors mean and one lady said yes.

We got Bibles for everyone and started explaining the verses but as I was going through the gospel, one at a time people started to leave. With each verse, someone else went inside their home. When these kinds of things happen, it really plays with your mind. I started thinking, "Man, I really suck at this!"

Finally, we got to the part where I asked if anyone wanted to receive the gift of salvation. There was one lady left with two of her kids, neither of whom were paying attention. I asked her if she would like the gift of eternal life that comes from confessing Christ's lordship and believing He was raised from the dead.

She said yes! Wow! She didn't go to church and was a single mom of four or five kids. When I asked about discipleship, she was thrilled to know someone would want to talk to her more about how to live for Jesus. What is also super fun, is that even a few days later, she was still excited about being discipled.

Listen! A farmer went out to plant some seed. As he scattered it across his field, some of the seed fell on a footpath, and the birds came and ate it. Other seed fell on shallow soil with underlying rock. The seed sprouted quickly because the soil was shallow. But the plant soon wilted under the hot sun, and since it didn't have deep roots, it died. Other seed fell among thorns that grew up and choked out the tender plants so they produced no grain. Still other seeds fell on fertile soil, and they sprouted, grew, and produced a crop that was thirty, sixty, and even a hundred times as much as had been planted! (Mark 4:3-8)

In my story there were people who were like the soil where the seed fell beside the road and the birds snatched it. A lot of them heard the prayer, read some of the verses, and received love from us. But a time came where what was sown was snatched, which is why the people left.

By the fifth verse that I shared, there was only one soil left. The good soil. I look forward to seeing what kind of crop comes because of her changed life. She could radically change her own community because she heard and understood the gospel and received the gift of eternal life.

I used to try so hard not to waste seed and only to sow into the "fertile soil," mostly because I wanted to see people saved. I didn't want to "waste" my time on those who wouldn't receive Christ. Then the Lord challenged me to look closer at this text. Never once when Jesus explains the parable did He criticize the sower for wasting his seed. It is never a waste to spend time and to sow the seed of the gospel into someone who might never receive it. The job of the sower, your job, is to sow the seed, not to determine what kind of soil you are sowing into.

Also, notice that the sower has no control over size of the crop. It would be nice if everyone we led to the Lord would choose to leave everything behind to follow Jesus and devote themselves to making disciples as well. Here we see that one out of four soils produces any kind of yield and even then, only one of the three yields mentioned is a hundred times as much as was planted.

There may be times when you lead someone to the Lord and they're going to affect a small number of people for the kingdom of God. Praise the Lord. Other times you're going to affect someone who will shift entire nations for the gospel. That's equally as amazing. Any increase is better than none! Even if there is no increase, the Lord is still good and worthy of praise.

We need to focus on the part that we can do something about. In this passage, Jesus is really just trying to motivate people to get to work and sow some seed. The seed has already been provided for you, so you don't have an excuse to wait for the shipment to arrive. Get out there and scatter some seed. Focus on your responsibility. Maybe for those of you who are OCD and need everything to be super perfect, you could line all your seed in a nice row on the ground, or carefully place each one on the soil. Either way, what matters is that you're doing something. It is my hope is that it will be a little more today than it was yesterday.

DAY 3
EAU CLAIRE, WI

YOUR PHONE IS NEVER FAST ENOUGH

I was on a team that decided to go to a park that also happened to have a zoo and a skate park all on the same property. When we pulled into the parking lot, there was a young man beside his car and a girl with a skateboard beside him. Immediately, my heart started beating like crazy. I knew we were supposed to talk to them. I didn't say anything right away and my team members wanted to see if anyone was by the entrance to the zoo. The further we got from them, the faster my heart beat. Nobody was by the zoo, so we turned around and I expressed the desire to talk with the guy and girl we'd seen.

We pulled back into the area where they had been and saw they were still hanging out. Two people from our team approached them and the other two of us stayed to pray. I was excited because I was pretty sure these kids needed to get saved. A few minutes later my teammates got back in the car.

Surprised that they hadn't been out there very long, I asked what happened. They explained that another team had already prayed for the kids, so our driver started to pull away. My heart sank because I knew we were supposed to talk to them, but it seemed like they didn't want to talk to us.

We headed to the skate park across the street, so that two of us could encounter the kids skateboarding. Another teammate and I were discussing what had happened with the guy and girl when all of a sudden, through the rear window I saw the guy riding a bike backwards toward us, and the girl riding her skateboard alongside! I was excited, so I got out of the car.

"What are you doing?" my teammate asked. "We already talked to them and we should leave them alone."

"I haven't talked to them yet," I responded.

As I approached the young man, I had my phone out and was trying to get my video to work as I called across the parking lot, "Hey hold on, don't do any cool tricks till I give you the signal!"

They laughed at me as the guy kept riding in reverse. My phone was finally working so I gave him the signal and he started to do all sorts of sweet tricks. The girl with him stopped by me and watched him do his cool moves. I told them that I had heard a rumor that some people had approached them earlier and asked if they could pray for them. They confirmed that two groups of people had in fact talked to them and one group prayed for them. I asked if anyone had given them a wristband, and they said no.

"What! They didn't give you a wristband?" I said, "I will harass them for that later."

I handed them the wristbands and asked if they'd like to know what the colors represent. They said they would, so we walked through the wristband and they both accepted the gift of salvation! We talked with them about discipleship and they were interested. The girl was willing to be discipled by a lady on my team, who just happened to be one of the two people who had originally talked to them!

Romans 8:14 says, "For all who are led by the Spirit of God are children of God." For some of you, the concept of being led by the Holy Spirit is new or maybe your doctrine doesn't believe in it.

There was a time in Muncie, Indiana when a guy sitting next to me at breakfast asked, "How do you know when the Holy Spirit is speaking to you?"

I thought about it and responded, "How do you know you have to go to the bathroom?"

He replied, "I don't know... I have a feeling."

I told him that in the same way your body tells you that you have to "go," the Lord often speaks to us through impressions that we feel in our bodies.

For example, let's say as a kid your parents told you not to watch R-rated movies. You end up at someone's house with a group of friends and they decide to watch this amazing new movie, but it's rated R. Something inside you is saying, "Warning! Warning! Your mom said not to watch this kind of movie." Then you have to make a decision to do it, or not to do it. It's the same way with the Holy Spirit.

Let's say you read the Bible and you see that it tells you to love your neighbor. And then you're walking by your neighbor and you get a goofy feeling and a thought comes to your head that you should go love this guy. Those feelings and thoughts are most likely the Holy Spirit. The Spirit's job is to empower you to live for Jesus and like Jesus. The Spirit is never going to tell you to sin, and will never say something in opposition of what you read in scripture as a command from the Lord.

In Romans we see that we are children of God when we are led by the Spirit. And Galatians 5:25 says, "Since we are living by the Spirit, let us follow the Spirit's leading in every part of our lives." I believe this is more than just a charge to live by the Spirit when it comes to holy living, but to allow the Spirit of God to lead every bit of your life, including, but not limited to, who to talk to or where to go when you're wanting to share the good news.

In Acts 10, Peter was on a roof spending some time alone in prayer. The Lord showed him the same vision three times to prepare him for what he was about to do.

> Meanwhile, as Peter was puzzling over the vision, the Holy Spirit said to him, "Three men have come looking for you. Get up, go downstairs, and go with them without hesitation. Don't worry, for I have sent them." (Acts 10:19-20)

Here we see an instance where the Spirit tells a man to do something practical, go downstairs and go with the guys who showed up at the door. In my story, I felt the Spirit leading me to talk to a specific guy and girl. Sometimes you will hear something and it won't make a ton of sense, but try it out, you never know what will happen. You need to allow the Holy Spirit to guide you to those whose hearts are ready so that they can be saved. Maybe you will have an opportunity to lead a whole family to Jesus, like Peter did at the end of the chapter. In verse 48, they even got baptized!

Today my encouragement to you is this: pray and ask the Lord to tell you to do something, and then be quiet. If you have a weird idea or you see a picture in your imagination or a song pops in your head or whatever, try it and see what happens. You never know. For me, I know when my heart beats fast and I feel like I have a frog in my throat, it's the Lord. I have seen it confirmed many times before. Just ask Jesus to help you understand what He's saying and He will.

DAY 4
CHAMPAIGN COUNTY, OH

DRIVING IN CIRCLES

This was one of those days that started to get a bit frustrating. My team had gone to the local skate park/playground and tried to interact with the people there and nobody wanted to talk to us. (I don't know why! We are such great people!) So we went someplace to get ice cream for our sons, who had come with us, and again there really wasn't anyone willing to converse with us. (If you're scared to share the gospel, just go for ice cream and see what happens! Maybe it will work for you.) We decided to cruise the town and see what might stand out.

Ohio has these amazing places the locals just call "the drive-through." They are drive-through convenience stores that primarily sell liquor, but they can have pizza, nachos, soda, and other stuff too. They look similar to a car wash, but with refrigerators on the inside. You have to drive through the building to purchase stuff instead of driving up to a window. I LOVE THEM! (Not because of the alcohol, they are just so unique.)

Anyways, as we were cruising through the town I happened to notice this one particular drive-through, because it was much smaller than the other ones I have seen, and on top of that, it was also smaller than the other stuff surrounding it.

When I first saw the drive-through I didn't say anything, but after we had gone to the fairgrounds and a few other places, I couldn't get it out of my mind. So we decided to go back. I have learned that if there is a place, person, or something that you can't get out of your mind, you should go there, or talk to them, or do whatever you need to do with that because there is a good chance the Lord is telling you to do it. Pray about it and ask yourself, "Would Jesus go here?" (I mean the real Jesus, not the made up American one. You know, the one that loves sinners and hangs out with whores and traitors.)

We pulled into the drive-through and asked if they had anything to drink that wasn't beer. We said we were new to Ohio and where we live the only drive-throughs are at fast food joints. The lady was kind to us, and we got Mountain Dew. When she gave us our drink, we asked her if and how we could pray for her.

Immediately, she said "Yes, my cousin was killed in a car accident two days ago."

Now, because this was a drive-through, we needed to be considerate to the cars behind us that are used to getting their alcohol and moving on, and we didn't want to hold up business. On top of that, we really didn't know where this girl was at in her relationship with Jesus. We prayed a quick thirty-second prayer for her, and just like we had been trained to do, we offered her a wristband as a way to remind her that we had prayed. She gladly accepted it.

I said, "Each color on the band stands for a specific word, would you like to know what that word is?"

She said yes, but a car pulled up behind us. So we asked, "If we pull forward and come back around would that be okay?"

She gave us permission, so we pulled out onto the main street, and then back around to the beginning. Another attendant came up to us, but we told him that we were there to see the lady that was working (which at first sounds really creepy...oh well). He smiled and went back into the office and the girl came back to us, also with a smile. This confirmed that we were not being as creepy as we felt.

We explained the first verse to her, which talks about how we all sin, and that's what the yellow part of the wristband represents. At this point another car or two had pulled in behind us, so we were all watching to make sure we weren't holding anyone up.

Then the lady read the second verse, which stands for death, but the car behind us was ready to go. Again we pulled out onto the street and, with her permission, came back through. She read the third verse, which stands for love. We chatted about what that particular verse means and explained that we believe the reason God sent us to the drive-through was specifically for her, because He loves her. She smiled really big. Then of course by that time another car had come, so we went around again.

By this time the other attendant wouldn't even approach our car, because he knew we were there for her. I asked her if she could get into trouble for just chatting with us, and she said no. We asked if we were the weirdest people who ever came through the drive-through and she said, "Oh no, you guys are refreshing."

What? Have you ever thought that maybe you could be refreshing just because you weren't there to hit on someone or buy booze, but to minister to them? What if the man at your local liquor store is waiting for someone to come in just to love on him? What if that lady serving you at Applebee's is waiting for kind words and a good tip from someone who truly loves her and doesn't expect anything in return?

We went through the blue verse and explained that it represents the word "faith." And again, there were more cars behind us. By this time our boys were getting excited in the back of the van. They had been watching a movie as we were driving, but it caught their attention that we kept going around in circles, so they stopped watching the movie to see what would happen.

The sixth time around we went through the green verse. Now, one of the things that I really love about our little blue TTR Bibles is that they make sharing the gospel so simple. On the back of the book there is a question written in bold letters that I love to use. It says, "Is there anything or anyone that would keep you from accepting the free gift of life in Jesus today?"

She told us nothing was in the way, so we asked if she wanted to open the gift of eternal life. She said, "Yes!"

We were so happy! Who would've ever thought that driving through a drive-through over and over would lead to someone giving their life to Christ?

We led her through a prayer and asked if she would be interested in someone from the community meeting with her to tell her more about Jesus and the Bible, and to help her grow in her faith, and she excitedly agreed. She even said she'd like to go to church with that person! (That rarely happens, just so you know. Most people have had bad experiences and don't want to go to church right away.) After eight times through the drive-through our young lady friend went from death to life.

It is not those who are healthy who need a physician, but those who are sick; I did not come to call the righteous, but sinners. (Mark 2:17, NASB)

This is Jesus' response to the religious leaders who were questioning why in the world He would spend His time with sinners. Jesus had been hanging out with tax collectors who, at the time, were considered traitors because they were "collaborating" with the enemy, the Roman Empire. Tax collectors were also known to cheat people by charging more than they should.

During Jesus' day, if you wanted to be a good Jew, there were groups of people you didn't hang out with. I am sure their moms told them something like, "Don't hang out with those guys or you'll be like them," and yet here we see Jesus hanging out with these worldly people.

I am convinced that Jesus would have had no problem going to a liquor store to love on someone. He didn't come to call the righteous, but sinners. This sort of means that you have to go to places where the sinners are. This means you might have to get out of your element. You might have to go somewhere you wouldn't normally hang out. Sure, share the gospel in your neighborhood, but also go places that aren't in your neighborhood.

Ask the Lord, "Where do the sinners live in my town? Where do the drug dealers and whores hang out? Where are the gang bangers and pimps? Where are the thieves and liars?" Let's grab a friend and go find those guys. There's a really good chance you're not going to run into them on a normal Sunday.

Please use wisdom and discernment in this. Don't go alone and don't try to go all Rambo and try to take down bad guys by yourself. But don't use fear as an excuse to get out of talking to unsavory characters either.

This may mean that the Lord leads you to someone at your local KFC, or while you're getting a $5 pizza. It doesn't necessarily mean that you have to risk your life, but think about it. Jesus risked His life and reputation to come to earth and allowed Himself to be nailed to a cross after being beaten relentlessly for us. We have to ask ourselves, "Is it worth it?" Would it be worth possibly getting mugged or murdered for the sake of someone having eternal life? Jesus went to them. I have decided to follow Jesus, and that means that I need to do the same.

Today as you're reading this, ask the Lord where you should go. If this part is a bit scary, don't worry, the Lord is super kind and mostly just excited that you're finally trying to do something. He's probably going to send you someone easy first. After you have been doing it a while, He may send you to shadier places, but again, you don't have to fear. Today, let's go hang out with sinners and tell them the good news.

DAY 5
BEMIDJI, MN

FOR HEAVEN'S SAKE, DO SOMETHING

Anyone who knows me well probably knows that I grew up watching old movies. John Wayne was my hero (and still is!). Cary Grant, Fred Astaire, Danny Kaye, Bob Hope, Katherine Hepburn, and Maureen O'Hara were regulars on our tv set. Every once in a while the Lord will use this feature about me when I am in an encounter.

We had just finished a thirty minute talk on a local radio station and my friend Steve and I wanted to use the time we had left before dinner to share the gospel. In Bemidji, The "Paul Bunyan" park is a popular destination (I dont know its real name, I just know there is a huge statue of Paul and Babe the Blue Ox), so we got in the baptism truck and decided to go there to see who we could find.

As we drove into the parking lot, a man came up to us saying, "Praise God, I have been praying for revival." I was all excited that someone else wanted to see revival as much as we did, so we invited him to join us. He said he couldn't, that he was busy, and just walked away. We tried to pray with him too, but he just kept saying, "Praise God, I have been praying for revival." We didn't really understand what was going on, so we parked the truck and started to walk around, looking for people to pray for.

I saw a young man out of the corner of my eye, and immediately I felt like I should talk to him, but there was another man with reviveMINNESOTA already talking to him. It seemed from his body language that he didn't really want to talk, and my heart sank. The guy from Revive is an amazing person and extremely effective on the street, so I figured there was no way on earth this kid was actually going to want us to encounter him.

We walked through the parking lot, and saw our "praying for revival" friend, standing by his car holding the roof in place. We smiled at him and kept moving. Who knows, maybe he was praying for us.

We walked up to the area with the giant statues and the young man I wanted to talk to was sitting by himself at a park table/bench/thing. I watched from afar as a few others from Revive approached him, and they all walked away after a minute or two, so I just kept thinking that this kid would definitely not want to talk to me.

A few feet away from me there was a man and his little girl, who looked about my daughter Mercy's age. She would run up to the Babe the Blue Ox statue, smack it, and run away giggling as if the ox was going to retaliate somehow. It was hysterical, and so I asked her dad how old she was. He told me she was two and I asked what her name was. It turns out her name was Daphne.

Well, well well! I just happen to have an awesome cousin named Daphne! Haha, now I am excited! There is also this movie I used to watch a long time ago called *Some Like it Hot*, with Jack Lemmon and Tony Curtis. Jack Lemmon's character calls himself Daphne as well!

I asked the man if he'd ever seen it, and he hadn't, so I explained that it's about these two guys who are trying to escape the mafia, so they dress up like women and join an all-girl's traveling band. So I am telling this to little Daphne's father, and the young man that I had wanted to talk to starts walking by, overheard me talking about this movie, and comes right up to us.

"Excuse me, were you just talking about a movie called *Some Like it Hot*?" he asked.

I said yes, and he began to tell me about his favorite part in the movie. We talked for a bit, and then Daphne and her dad said goodbye and left the park. This young man and I kept talking about old movies, where he works, what he does for fun, really anything I could find out about him. Finally after we had talked for a long time, he asked me, "What do you like to do?"

I explained that I have four kids and that I love to spend time and do silly things with them. I also told him about how for fun, I really love to give people these wristbands, and I took one off my wrist and handed it to him. He loved it and excitedly asked me to explain it.

We went through the gospel and one thing he said that really stood out to me was that his father was Christian and his mom was Jewish. They had both decided not to push either faith on him but to let him decide what he believes.

I asked him the question on the back of the Bible, "Is there anything or anyone keeping you from accepting the free gift of life in Jesus today?" I love that question, because it keeps things simple for me. He said that nothing was keeping him, so I said, "Would you like to?"

He said YES! I led him through a prayer and he was so excited when we finished. We talked about the orange tab, focusing on discipleship, and he said that his dad would really love to disciple him. I agreed that dads are the best at that.

One of the most common things we see all across America, in every state we go to, are Christians who tell us they have been praying for revival. Yes! Keep praying, but at some point, you need to put shoes on your prayers and do something about it. The answer to the prayer "God, send revival," is you. Jesus already commissioned you. You have all the authority and power you need to accomplish the task He gave you.

We have to add works to our faith. Faith is what causes us to pray, and to a certain degree praying is a form of works, but the truth is that at some time we have to go forth and make disciples. They aren't going to be made on their own.

So you see, faith by itself isn't enough. Unless it produces good deeds, it is dead and useless.
Now someone may argue, "Some people have faith; others have good deeds." But I say, How can you show me your faith if you don't have good deeds? I will show you my faith by my good deeds."
You say you have faith, for you believe that there is one God. Good for you! Even the demons believe this, and they tremble in terror. How foolish! Can't you see that faith without good deeds is useless? (James 2:17-20)

We have to stop assuming that people are saved solely through our prayers. People are saved because we go forth and share the gospel. We have to give people the opportunity to accept the greatest gift of all. Yes, pray for revival, but for the sake of the lost, be revival to someone. Go bring the dead to life in Jesus' name. Go walk out the Great Commission that Jesus gives in Matthew 28:19-20.

Therefore, go and make disciples of all nations, baptizing them in the name of the Father and the Son and the Holy Spirit. Teach these new disciples to obey all the commands I have given you. And be sure of this: I am with you always, even to the end of the age.

Today before you leave the toilet, or wherever you are when you read this, ask the Lord who you can share you faith with. Whatever names come to mind, go talk to them. Maybe no name comes to mind, and a place does. Go there and look for someone, anyone, and find something to connect over, and share your faith.

RESPONSE

DAY 6
FORT WAYNE, IN

RACIAL UNITY

Have you ever gone out to share the gospel, but it seemed like everything that could go wrong, did go wrong? My family and I often travel together to different cities where Revive has already been to encourage the locals to continue going out. One trip was to Fort Wayne, Indiana where we had the privilege of joining the crew on a Wednesday evening. Just an FYI, our encounters are more fruitful at night than during the day (in my opinion). (Totally unverified.) (We might need to talk to the FBI and see if that is statistically correct.)

My three older children, Josiah (7), Gideon (5), and Mercy (3) came on my team, and we decided to go to a park. (Whenever kids are on my team, I try to go to a playplace or a park.) Of course this was one of those nights where my kids had already been in the car for a while and they were totally ready to run around like monkeys.

We ended up at a local park and not even five minutes after we got there, Gideon burst into screams! He had been stung by a bee! Right then, Mercy came running up, chanting that she had to poop.

I grabbed Gideon and began to pray for him, and of course he just wanted mommy. I looked around for a public bathroom hoping that there was something for Mercy to use.

One of the ladies on my team had some essential oils with her and we gave Gideon some of that. Then we went to the park office and the workers gave me an "ice pack" for Gideon (it was a latex glove filled with water and then frozen.) I took Mercy to the toilet while trying to calm Gideon down. I had just gotten him to stop screaming when Mercy came out with that plastic cover thing from the urinal! She was trying to tell me someone left it! Everything inside of me just wanted to head home. Nothing was going to plan.

I finally got Gideon to calm down by letting him bust the ice glove. Mercy finished and we headed to the play set. Josiah was hanging out with the rest of my team and had been warning all the kids that came onto the property where the bees were.

At last, everything started to relax. The kids were playing and my team engaged a few people. After a while there were only two little girls left playing with my kids. They were sisters, and happened to be Black. The kids were all chasing each other and giggling, as if they didn't have a clue how much tension there is in America between races. In their world, everything was fine. They were just playing with other kids. Race had nothing to do with it.

I looked around to find their parents, but there wasn't anyone sitting or standing near the playground, so I began to scan for someone in a car, and that's when I saw a woman watching them play. A specific phrase kept going through my mind so I decided to go up to this woman and see what would happen.

I walked up to the vehicle and asked the her if the little girls were hers and she said yes. I said, "You know it's crazy that fifty years ago, or more, our kids wouldn't have been able to do this."

She nodded and we began to talk about how much of a blessing it is that our kids don't have to grow up in a environment where they are encouraged not to play with kids of a different race. Even today there is still racial tension in places around the country, but there doesn't have to be. We all bleed the same color.

We introduced ourselves and we talked about our kids for a few minutes and, as it turns out, it was her daughter's birthday. While we were talking, one of her daughters fell off the play set and so we ran to check on her. She allowed our team to pray for her head, which she had hit pretty hard as she fell. After making sure the little girl was alright, we gave them wristbands and asked if they'd like to know what the colors mean. They did, so we walked them through it.

Halfway through, the kids decided they'd rather play tag again, and we had the opportunity to lead the mom to Jesus. She agreed to be discipled by one of the ladies on our team. It was super cool that was her daughter's birthday. Now her spiritual birthday is the same as her daughter's physical birthday!

Psalms 86:9 says this, "All the nations you made will come and bow before you, Lord; they will praise Your holy name." All nations will one day bow before the Lord. They will praise His holy name. That is so exciting to me.

All the racial tension in this world is exhausting. We figure out every possible way to hate each other. When I was a kid, I didn't grow up around a lot of minorities. Or so I thought. Why? My parents never talked about it. Not because they didn't think we should know and they wanted to hide it from us, but because they didn't see race as an issue. People were just people. I was taught to treat everyone the same. Be fair, be honest, and love everyone, no matter how much they irritate you. My parents didn't care if you were handicapped or what color your skin was. They only saw people.

When I was in high school my parents had me sit down to watch a movie called "Guess Who's Coming to Dinner," starring Spencer Tracy and Katharine Hepburn. We loved old movies! This 1967 film is about a young couple hosting a dinner to inform their parents of their engagement... and they are interracial. It shows the tensions and the surprises that come with dating other races. It is a really great film, but I was confused as to why I needed to watch it. My dad then explained that it was okay if I wanted to date a Black girl, and that they would support me if I chose to do that.

In some ways it is super cool that my parents did that, but I was so confused. I never would have EVER thought it would be a problem to date someone of a different race. I didn't know that there were people today who still got upset at that. As far as I knew it was a thing of the past, but I remember them telling me that there was some tension when they dated because they were not the same race.

When I had to start filling out forms for FAFSA and for other scholarship information, I kept seeing this line that asked if I was White, Hispanic, Black, or Asian. As a teenager I literally didn't know what to put, so I asked my mom. She told me that I am half German (on my dad's side) and half Mexican (on my mom's side). I didn't even know that "caca" was a Spanish word until then! Race was never talked about because it didn't matter. I was thrilled to know that I was part Mexican.

In Ephesians 2, Paul reminds the Gentiles (anyone who isn't a Jew) that at one point in time they were royally screwed. How so? They weren't allowed to be citizens in the kingdom of God because the covenant that God had made was with the people of Israel. This covenant was represented in their flesh through circumcision. But God fulfilled the old way of doing things through Jesus and made a way for both Jews and Gentiles to be close to Him, allowing for the racial divide to be closed, making peace between them.

> You lived in this world without God and without hope. But now you have been united with Christ Jesus. Once you were far away from God, but now you have been brought near to Him through the blood of Christ.
> For Christ Himself has brought peace to us. He united Jews and Gentiles into one people when, in His own body on the cross, He broke down the wall of hostility that separated us. (Eph. 2:12-14)

According to this passage, every Gentile that has been born again has been united into one people with the Jews. There is no longer a difference when we're in the presence of God. Sure, we are all unique and each race or ethnicity has things that make us different. God delights in our differences and He loves each nation He created. When we honor and love those whose skin tone and upbringing is different than our own something powerful takes place. Even though we are so unique, we have one great similarity: our need for a savior.

Paul continues, "Now all of us can come to the Father through the same Holy Spirit because of what Christ has done for us" (v. 18). When we are born again, we are united into one people, and the walls that were there before are destroyed by the blood of Jesus. Peace is now allowed to take place between nations and skin colors because Jesus took those walls and broke them down. No more should there be hostility in the body of Christ when it comes to race. Because we all have the same Holy Spirit, we can rejoice together instead of fighting about our petty differences.

Isaiah also prophesied about this, while declaring both the current glory of the Lord alongside details of the future.

> In Jerusalem, the Lord of Heaven's Armies
>   will spread a wonderful feast
>   for all the people of the world.
> It will be a delicious banquet
>   with clear, well-aged wine and choice meat.
> There He will remove the cloud of gloom,
>   the shadow of death that hangs over the earth.
> He will swallow up death forever!
>   The Sovereign Lord will wipe away all tears.
> He will remove forever all insults and mockery
>   against His land and people.
> The Lord has spoken! (Isa. 25:6-8)

What a day we have to look forward to. Not only are all the nations going to bow before the Lord, but we will all come together and have a party. One day in Jerusalem I will be able to dine with Africans and Asians and Australians and instead of the focus being on race, we will be focused on the Sovereign Lord! It will be a great day to celebrate, and the things that have divided people for years will pale in the sight of He who has conquered death.

I love that my kids don't have to grow up worrying that if they play with a Black kid someone will get lynched. My heart goes out to my brothers and sisters in Christ that are Black. I love you guys.

All nations will bow. My Asian brothers, my Hispanic brothers, my African brothers are all going to bow before one Lord and exalt one name. I look forward to that day.

Some of you don't live in a diverse area, so you may need to pray and ask the Lord to send you a friend who is different than you. Let's be intentional today to be kind to everyone regardless of ethnicity. And as we are kind, let's expect our hearts to melt together. Maybe you will get a chance to share the gospel!

DAY 7
BEMIDJI, MN/TUPELO, MS

WHAT'S HOLDING YOU BACK?

BEMIDJI, MN

Our ministry often teaches that it can take between twelve and sixteen times of sharing the gospel with someone before they make the decision to follow Christ. I don't think it's provable, but again our friends at the FBI might disagree. If this is even partly true, you don't really know where a person is at when you meet them. It's not like they have a sign on their forehead with a gospel tally, marking how many they have left. You just have to go for it, and see where they land.

This particular day we decided to take some teams out at night and I was driving the baptism truck. A few of us needed to be back at the host church before the rest of the people showed up, so we decided to go together. As we were leaving, we saw a family outside their house about a block north of the church. We almost drove off, but then a little girl said she wanted to get baptized. All three of us ended up talking individually with someone from the family about the gospel. I was sharing with the mother.

She told me that some of her sons and daughters had already been baptized earlier that week. As I shared the gospel with her, I could tell that she really wanted to believe the message, but something was holding her back. Finally, I asked her what it was, and she said, "Myself."

She began to tell me about how she was a Native American and believed the traditional teachings of her tribe. I prayed with her and asked the Lord to open her eyes. She said that part of her was really excited for her kids, because she saw the changes in them, but that she still wasn't ready to give her life to Christ. I asked if I could pray with her one more time, and she agreed. She began to cry and her husband called over to her that they all needed to leave, but not before the other two guys on my team were able to lead two more of her daughters to the Lord and baptize them right there in front of their house!

It is always hard when someone says no to the gospel, but it is my hope that one day we will see her in heaven, because her children continue sharing the good news with her in word and deed.

TUPELO, MS

As your heart is beginning to break for the lost, you have to ask yourself if you are willing to be rejected or ignored. When we arrived in Tupelo, we were informed that everyone in the deep south is a Christian so we would be only going out to bless the community, and sharing the gospel wouldn't be very common.

As we often do while we are out driving around asking the Lord to show us where to go and who to talk to, my team noticed a woman washing her car in her driveway. Since in some neighborhoods it is frowned upon to pull up in front of a house and jump out of a van, we pulled ahead and parked down the street a bit. Two of us walked back toward the lady washing her car, and as we walked, we prayed that the Lord would use us.

As we got closer to her driveway, she noticed us and greeted us right away. This often means that the person is comfortable enough to allow us to come closer. We started to chit chat about her car and the weather and how it was a great day to wash a car. She asked if we lived in the neighborhood, and was excited to know I am from Indiana. (Apparently, Hoosiers don't go to Tupelo much.)

After a while, we asked how her we could pray for her and she excitedly gave us her request. She stopped washing her car and, like most people in the south, joined us by holding our hands.

There we were in public, holding hands and praying for this woman, and I felt like we had the go ahead to share more with her. We offered her the wristband and she readily accepted it. She began to look at it and read the words on it, and so we asked if she had a minute so we could explain the colors.

She gave us permission to proceed. I was thrilled as we talked through each passage because it was very clear she had an amazing grasp on all the verses. I could tell she had grown up in church, but she'd mentioned that she didn't go anymore. At the very end when we asked if there was anything that would keep her from accepting the free gift, she said, "No, nothing is in the way."

I was so excited! "Nothing is in the way!" I thought. "Surely she is going to get saved!"

So we asked her if she would like to accept the gift of life, and she said no.

I was shocked. She understood the texts so well! Nothing was in the way! Why wouldn't you want the gift that leads to eternal life? She explained that she understood what she was saying and that she was okay with it. I was heartbroken and speechless.

She picked up her hose to continue washing her car, thanked us for dropping by, and said if we were ever in those parts again to give her a visit. We thanked her for her time and for allowing us to explain the Bible, and we blessed her as we walked away.

This was the first time for me in an encounter where the person blatantly understood the passages, knew the ins and outs of all of it, and just flat out didn't want it. She wasn't rude, or angry, or bitter. She just didn't want to be saved.

The truth we all have to face is this. People will go to hell. If there is anything I can do through the power of the Spirit to convince someone to choose Christ then I will do it, but there have been many times when I have walked away from an encounter with someone, and I know in my heart that God met them there, yet they still walked away unsaved. This breaks my heart. But you can't allow people's rejection of the gospel stop you from continuing to share. We aren't responsible for their decisions, but we are responsible for giving them the opportunity to make one.

> For this is how God loved the world: He gave His one and only Son, so that everyone who believes in Him will not perish but have eternal life. God sent His Son into the world not to judge the world, but to save the world through Him.
> There is no judgment against anyone who believes in Him. But anyone who does not believe in Him has already been judged for not believing in God's one and only Son." (John 3:16-18)

Not every encounter is going to end with someone being born again. What breaks my heart is that these people are condemned already, according to John. They have chosen not to believe the one He sent.

Who do you know that is not saved? Does it bother you to know that you have friends and family going to hell? They don't have to. There is hope for them. Nobody is too far gone. Jesus came so that they might be saved. Ask the Lord before you leave your house for the day, "Who do I know that I need to share the love of Jesus with today?"

You don't need our wristband to love someone. You don't need our cool Bible that makes everything easy. You only need the Holy Spirit and He will guide you. Just remember this: Love never fails. It says so in 1 Corinthians 13. Join the apostles in this prayer, "Give us, your servants, great boldness in preaching your word." (Acts 4:29) These guys were being threatened when they prayed these words. They knew that they could very well be murdered for sharing the gospel, but instead of backing down they prayed for boldness to preach the good news.

You have the lion of the tribe of Judah living inside you, not a coward. What is inside you gives you power, love, and a sound mind, not the license to cower. Ask the Lord to show you the people you know who are going to hell and you have never told them they didn't have to, and then talk to them. Don't judge them. That's not your job. Love them.

DAY 8
SOMEWHERE IMPORTANT, USA

MY HOPE

Today instead of a story, I would like to encourage you with a few thoughts. Your Father in heaven wants to know you. If you read through the Bible like most people read through any other book, you will see one massive story about a God who is nuts about His creation. No matter which knucklehead is screwing everything up, we still find Him there, figuring out ways for us to get to know Him.

If we look at the garden of Eden, we see that God walked with man. Why? Because He wanted us to know Him. He's all-knowing. He doesn't need us to tell him anything, and yet He models how to show love to those around us, by being present and conversing, asking questions that you already know the answers to. Then when everything gets jacked up, we still see God chatting with Adam and Eve and their descendants throughout the Old Testament.

Way before Jesus ever became flesh, God had been doing what was necessary for mankind to know Him. Most people hate the sacrificial system of Leviticus and the craziness of Judges, yet even in the strangest books of the Bible, we see a common story. Men and women act like fools and God shows up to save the day. He is the hero.

It is my hope that, even though I am telling these stories from my perspective, you will see that I am nothing more than a tool in the hand of an amazing God. On my own I can save no one. Jesus was with God in the beginning, and everything that has been made is for Him. That includes us. People with skin and bones were made by Jesus and for Jesus.

Time and time again we see Jesus going incredibly out of His way to hang out with people, knowing full well that we are selfish, manipulative, liars, adulterers, making idol after idol, our hearts rarely focusing on Him, and He still chooses to love us. He is crazy.

We do not deserve His love, which compels me all the more to share it with everyone I know. Why would He love me? I am a mess! I often don't do what I ought (Paul said it too, so don't send me letters in the mail).

Even though I am a mess, I find myself wanting to be more and more like Him. He inspires me to do what He asks of me, no matter how difficult the task, because there was a day that He decided to become incarnate and live a life on this earth so that I could have eternal life. He paid the debts I couldn't pay, and it makes me long to serve him better.

Please don't read this and think to yourself, "Oh, but Jesse is so bold, he can do things I can't."

The truth is that I have something inside me called the Holy Spirit, and if you're a true Christian you do too. I made Jesus my Lord which means that I have to do what He says, and what's weird is that I WANT to do it too because I know I will get to see something awesome.

When I was a kid I would hear stories about what God was doing in other places, and I would be jealous. That jealousy provoked me to jump all in for Jesus. I don't want to just hear stories of God doing amazing things, I WANT TO BE THERE.

Recently I read a cool story in 1 Samuel 7 where God speaks through thunder, causing confusion among the Philistines, and the Israelites kick their Philistine butts because they were running around like chickens with their heads cut off. I want to see God show up like that for me!

And let us run with endurance the race that is set before us, fixing our eyes on Jesus, the author and perfecter of faith, who for the joy set before Him endured the cross, despising the shame, and has sat down at the right hand of the throne of God." (Heb. 12:1-2, NASB)

Listen, keep your eyes on Jesus as you read these stories. Don't get caught up in silly, flawed people like me who are going to let you down. Follow Jesus, the author and perfecter of faith. The King James Version says "finisher" of our faith. I like that wording because it shows me that He invented our faith and He finishes it.

People like me will screw it up eventually, but if your eyes are on Jesus, you're not going to be fazed when I do screw up. Sure, I love the passage that says "And you should imitate me, just as I imitate Christ" (1 Cor. 11:1). But even if you imitate me your eyes should still be on Jesus.

DAY 9
MARSHFIELD, WI

LET'S GO TO THE MAGIC STORE

*At the advice of much wiser men than I, the names of the people that we encounter in this story have been changed to protect their identities.

My heart is to share the gospel. This may sound bad, but if I haven't recently led someone to the Lord, I start to get antsy. I love to minister to the body of Christ, don't get me wrong, but to me there is nothing more fulfilling than to watch someone go from death to life in front of your eyes. I love to rejoice with the angels as we glorify Jesus for the work that He did on the cross, conquering death and the grave so that we can have eternal life.

This was one of those days. I hadn't led anyone to the Lord that week. My friend Garrett and I ended up in the restroom at the same time after lunch, and I said to him, "Man, Garrett, would you go on a team with me? I am kind of getting tired of praying with Christians. I need to lead someone to the Lord."

That may sound weird to some of you, but it's where I was at that day, right or wrong.

"Someone has been asking me to go to this witchcraft store all week," Garrett said. "Maybe we should go there this afternoon?"

"Yeah! For sure the magic store will have someone who needs to get saved," I said giddily, like a schoolboy.

We found Hank and Alonie, these two amazing locals that we trusted to go with us, and went to the magic store. Before we went in, we prayed over each other and asked the Lord if this is what His will was for us, or if we should be going somewhere else. We all felt the okay to head inside, so we did. We moseyed around the shop looking around at different things. I walked up to three people, two sitting at a table, and the other was facing them sitting in the aisle.

The one sitting in the aisle was wearing chains and a leather vest, sunglasses in a dark room, and had tattoos all over. His beard was black and really long like ZZ Top and his hair was even longer, almost down to his butt. His name was Jack. The other two were the store owner and her daughter. The daughter's name was Brittany.

After we had been talking for a while, Brittany and Jack got up to go outside to smoke. Garrett and I followed them. As soon as my feet hit the cement on the sidewalk outside the door, I felt the Lord say, "You're here for her."

Paying attention to her body language and the conversation, I didn't think I'd ever get to talk to her. She was interacting a lot with my other teammates, but wasn't really talking to me, so I kept talking to Jack. She finished smoking and went back inside the store, and I just kept waiting for my opportune time.

Jack and I had been talking a long time, but when Brittany came out again, she gave me a side hug and thanked us for being so kind and nice. She said she was sorry, but she had to get to work. I said, "Look, this is going to sound really off the wall, and probably a bit weird, but I don't know how else to say it, so I will just throw it out there and see what happens."

She said, "Okay, what is it?"

"When we all came outside earlier, as soon as my foot hit the cement, the Lord told me that we were here for you."

That was literally all I knew at that point. What happened next was as if the Lord just spoke right through me. I wasn't even thinking this until it came out.

"There's something you're going through that you haven't told anyone. I don't know if I can say for sure that you're ashamed of it, but either way you haven't told anyone what it is. Nobody knows. Is that true?"

She nodded that it was.

"Would you like to be free from that?"

"Yes," she said.

I said, "Well, let's get out of the way and move over a bit."

We called Garrett out of the store, and he joined us in front of the next store over that looked as if it was empty. (Just an FYI, I never pray with a woman alone. There is always a second person with me.)

There we were, standing downtown in front of an empty store with cars constantly passing by us. We asked her if she would be brave enough to tell us what it was. She confided in us, and Garrett said, "That's why you haven't been baptized isn't it?"

I didn't know that the two of them had talked inside the store and already discussed everything I had just told her. He had also asked if she had been baptized and she said no. Then the Lord showed him that because of what she was dealing with, she felt she couldn't get baptized. We prayed for the Lord to release her from what she was struggling with, and while I prayed I felt the need to tell her something.

"You know, being tempted to do something isn't wrong. Jesus was tempted, and yet knew no sin. So it isn't wrong to be tempted, it's only wrong to act on it. Your body can crave something it shouldn't, but we have to say 'no' when those times come."

All of a sudden, in my mind I saw a hand with three fingers up, and I knew exactly what it meant. I asked her, "How much time do you have until you absolutely have to leave or you'll be late?"

"Fifteen minutes."

I told her that I felt like there was someone she needed to forgive. She said yes, so I asked if we could lead her in a prayer through that. She agreed.

"Who is it you need to forgive?" I asked.

"Myself," she said.

So we led her through a prayer forgiving herself, releasing her from the need to be good enough and from not measuring up. Then I asked if there was anyone else and she said her dad. So we led her through a prayer forgiving her dad. I asked her if there was anyone else and she said no. But I had seen three fingers, not two, so I asked again. "Are you sure there is nobody else?"

She said, "Yeah, but I can't forgive him."

"You *can't* forgive him, or you *won't* forgive him?"

After a pause, she admitted, "Won't."

I looked at the time and told her, "I can't make you forgive. I know we don't have much time left," it was three minutes to be exact, "but can I share something real quick?"

I told her about the parable Jesus told in Matthew 18 where this one guy gets forgiven a huge sum and then refuses to forgive someone else who begs mercy for a tiny sum. It says at the end of that passage that the guy who didn't show mercy was taken and thrown into a prison to be tortured day and night.

"This is what happens when we choose not to forgive, whether it's physical, spiritual or emotional, either way you're tortured. On top of that, the last verse of that passage says that if we don't forgive others, our heavenly Father won't forgive us," I said. "Look, I can't make you forgive this guy, but you have a choice to make. Either you can go to work today bound up because you choose not to forgive, or you can go set free. What do you want to do?"

She said, "Okay," then grabbed our hands and began to forgive a guy named Jesse.

I was shocked! How crazy is it that God would send someone named Jesse to a person who needed to forgive someone named Jesse, just so that she could release that unforgiveness and be set free. Jesus loves us so much, He's willing to call us out in whatever way necessary to get us freed up.

As soon as she was done praying she had to go. She took off to her car and yelled back at us that she would be coming the next morning to the reviveWisconsin outreach. And she did! She came into the church around breakfast time, smiling ear to ear!

"You won't believe it," she said. "Last night was the first time I can remember not having any nightmares!"

"Praise God!" I said. "Because you forgave others, look what happened!"

We got to take her out on the streets later that day, and she ended up getting baptized! God is good!

In a letter that Paul wrote to the Corinthian church, he teaches them about spiritual gifts and how to use them.

> A spiritual gift is given to each of us so we can help each other. To one person the Spirit gives the ability to give wise advice; to another the same Spirit gives a message of special knowledge. (1 Cor. 12:7-8)

I could go on with this passage because it's super great, but I want to focus here on the reality that a gift is given by the Holy Spirit to be able to give a message of special knowledge. Some versions call it the gift of "words of knowledge."

What happens is this. The Lord, who knows EVERYTHING, gives you knowledge or insight about a person that would be impossible for you to find out on your own. It can be someone you do or do not know, but according to verse 7 the point of the gift is so that we can help each other, build each other up in the faith, to "edify" one another.

In the encounter with Brittany, the Lord gave me a message of special knowledge: that I was there for her. When I released what I knew, the Lord released the rest. I knew something I couldn't have known because the Lord, who knows everything about everyone, chose to tell me. The Spirit wants to give us insights so that people will come to know the Lord.

I know this passage is saying that to "one" He gives one gift and to another a different gift, but it was through one Spirit that they were all distributed. This is true. There are many gifts and the Giver disperses them to whom He chooses. If you want to operate with any gift of the Spirit, spend time with Jesus. Don't just go to church services, but spend time reading the Word and praying. "Draw near to God and He will draw near to you" (James 4:8, NASB).

Honestly, the point of learning God's voice, both for the purpose of sharing the gospel or just for making decisions at home, is intimacy with Jesus. The more we obey his voice, the closer we get to Jesus. He wants to tell us what He thinks of us just much as He wants to use us to share the gospel.

I encourage you to ask for the gifts of the Spirit, because they will help you in every area of life, especially when you're sharing the gospel. Take the time to listen for the Spirit's leading/prompts and respond to them. Also, don't feel like something is broken in you if you don't hear anything after you've tried. It doesn't mean that Jesus loves you less or anything. It just means you didn't hear. Keep going for it and see what happens.

The point of any gift of the Spirit is not to help us become cool or famous, but to help us glorify our Father in heaven and love our neighbors through them. Do NOT get caught in the trap that makes you believe you're super great and better than others because the Spirit gave you a gift. You weren't given a gift so that you can glorify yourself, but that God will be glorified and the hearer encouraged.

Today, I want you to practice this. Listen for the Spirit's guidance while you're at work, going to school, or going to the movies. If you notice someone, ask the Lord to show you something about that person in particular, something that you couldn't know or deduce on your own, so that the Lord receives glory from it and so that people will be encouraged.

When He shows or tells you something, have the courage to release it. You can tell the person that you make mistakes, but that you're practicing and you wanted to know if this (insert message here) means anything to that person. Try it today.

RESPONSE

DAY 10
MARSHFIELD, WI

$#@%&

I'd like to continue the story from yesterday so that you know what happened aside from our encounter with Brittany.

If you remember, Jack and I had been talking inside prior to his going outside to smoke. I went with him and we talked about all kinds of things. He told me about how he was making this leather jacket on his own. He was going to put saw blades on the collar and spikes all over it. We talked about how he used to do all of these adrenaline rush activities, like walking on coals and stuff like that.

After a while, I gave him the wristband, and we went through the colors. He told me about how he had tried to live for Jesus when he was a kid, but had rebelled so much, and was so far gone, that he knew he couldn't be saved. He came up with excuse after excuse of how he was too bad of a person. That was when Brittany walked up and we went to pray.

My teammates had kept the conversation going with him while Garrett and I were praying with Brittany, so when I returned they were still talking about spiritual things. I knew what time it was and that we needed to start wrapping things up and get to the church for our evening duties. Finally, I challenged Jack's "man card."

"Man, you have been telling us about how you like to do all this crazy stuff for the rush. If you want a real rush, I dare you to come to the church tonight and pray with us."

"What time?" he asked.

So we told him what time the service started and he agreed to come with us. We got in the car and he followed our team to the church. When we got there, I had a text that they needed one more person to pray with a lady. Man! I wanted to be with Jack!

As I prayed about what I was supposed to do, I felt the Lord release me to pray with the lady. "Garrett and Hank have got this" was running through my mind. What happens next is what I have gathered from them.

During dinner Hank and Garrett kept talking with our bearded friend while I was in my prayer session. Finally, Garrett asked what was keeping him from making a commitment to Christ. He gave some more excuses, so Garrett and Hank helped him work through them. Finally he said he wanted to be born again.

They prayed with him and the three of them went outside. They showed him the baptism truck, and asked if he wanted to get baptized. He gave every excuse in the world as to why not. Earlier in their conversation though, Jack had been talking about how men who can't or won't do as they should are pussies. (I am leaving that in there because you need to understand what we were dealing with. He wasn't opposed to speaking his mind or using profanity.)

So Garrett said, "Why don't you just stop being a pussy, and get baptized?"

"You know, you're right," he said.

He grabbed a change of clothes from the bins that we have in the truck so people can get baptized without getting their own clothes wet. Garrett was able to get the truck going and the team live-streamed into the church as Garrett and Hank baptized Jack.

Whenever someone gets baptized, the place goes wild! Well, because they had done it in the truck outside instead of inside the church, Jack hadn't seen the response. They went into the sanctuary to join the service and sat in the front row. Kyle (the leader of TTR who oversees the services) was nearby, so Hank told him, "You know,

Jack wasn't inside to hear the warm welcome he got for joining the kingdom of God."

So Kyle got up, introduced him, and the place ERUPTED! He didn't know what to do because he had never received anything like that before. I saw him that night after the service and the guys told me all that had happened. I rejoiced with them!

The next day, Jack showed up to the evening service. He was dressed in a tucked-in grey shirt, without the leather jacket. And he was smiling like crazy, which he hadn't done the entire time we were with him the day before, until he got saved.

I was supposed to pray with a group again, but there was a misunderstanding and they ended up praying with a different crew than the one I was part of. Jack, Garrett, a woman named Susan from our prayer ministry, and I were standing in the foyer.

Susan was also supposed to have been praying with the other group, so she said to Jack, "Hey, since our people backed out, we should pray with you!"

Garrett and I said, "Yeah, that would be cool!" Jack shrugged his shoulders as if it wasn't a big deal, but he agreed to pray with us.

As we prayed with him Susan received a word of knowledge and released it to him. We ended up praying with him for two hours. He had to work the next day, but because he could feel his life changing, he didn't want to leave.

The next day when Garrett and I were driving back home from Wisconsin, Garrett got a call from Jack. When he answered, the first thing he heard was, "How the @#$%& @#$%#& @#$$%& did you guys know that?"

Garrett told him that sometimes when we're praying for people, the Holy Spirit will tell us something about that person just to show how much He knows them and that He really does care. Jack told us about how he went to work the next day and was telling everyone that our team might be psychics because we told him about something that four people in the whole world knew, and there was no way on earth these people who were new to town would know that about him.

Recently, I was able to talk with Hank (who has been discipling Jack) and he told me that they meet every Tuesday, have been going to this men's Bible study together, and Jack has really been getting a lot out of it. After I left, he had been fired from his job because he couldn't keep up, because he has carpal tunnel. Trying to figure out how or why God would let something like that happen to him, he called Garrett and Hank for help. Now, a few months later, he has a new job that doesn't mess with his carpal tunnel and he is loving it!

Hank told him, "Maybe God wanted you to have a better job that you would be better at, so that you wouldn't destroy your body. Maybe what you thought was a curse was really a blessing."

Many of you reading this haven't been able to get past the fact that I wrote a word in here that you were taught is naughty. Sure, I understand the passages that say, "Don't use foul or abusive language" (Eph. 4:29) and whatnot. My goal isn't to use profanity around every corner, but to help you understand a truth. People who aren't saved use profanity. They don't have to clean up their language because they aren't being held to the standard set forth in the Bible for Christian living. But you're not upset that Jack said it, you're upset that a member of the team said it, and that I chose to write it.

Here is my reason why. Language is important in conveying a message. Jack used that word a lot, and Garrett needed to get the point across in a way that he would understand. Jack's story is powerful, I am honored to be a part of this man's changed life, and I am honored to be in ministry with Garrett, who is willing to break free from religious man-made rules to reach a man who was lost.

There is a beautiful story in the book of John about a woman who was caught in the middle of the mess that she created for herself. While in the very act of committing a sin that by law was punishable by death, she was taken from her lover's arms and brought to the feet of Jesus. In that moment, her accusers began to slander her in front of a crowd, bringing evidence of her guilt.

As these religious leaders ripped her to shreds, Jesus began to write on the ground. Frustrated that He would be consumed by petty things like playing in the dirt when the law needed to be carried out, the accusers demanded Jesus' attention to the matter. Guilty! She absolutely was, and the law required her to be stoned to death. Jesus then stood to address the crowd.

"All right, but let the one who has never sinned throw the first stone!" Then He stooped down again and wrote in the dust.

When the accusers heard this, they slipped away one by one, beginning with the oldest, until only Jesus was left in the middle of the crowd with the woman.

Then Jesus stood up again and said to the woman, "Where are your accusers? Didn't even one of them condemn you?"

"No, Lord," she said.

And Jesus said, "Neither do I. Go and sin no more." (John 8:7-11)

We all need to remember that there are moments in each of our lives when we've done something that we wish we hadn't. Some of us have even done things that, according to "the law of the land," deserve death. And we are absolutely GUILTY. Yet there is a man who has the audacity to not condemn you, even though He has every right to.

What I love about this passage is that Jesus was the only one who had the right to throw stones and instead, He extended mercy. There is no record of her even asking for it (though it doesn't mean she didn't) and yet that is what is given. Death was deserved but she was given the gift of life.

Another observation here is that the entire story, while it seems to be about Jesus and an adulteress woman, is also about religious people trying to trap Jesus. They looked for someone they could use to prove their point, regardless of the damage it did. People's lives were being transformed by Jesus, and the Pharisees couldn't stand the fact that He didn't fit into the mold they wanted.

They couldn't let this man destroy everything they knew was true. They couldn't let this man destroy their way of living and their values, so they needed to prove to the world how wrong He was. Yet in their attempt, Jesus exposed their hearts and proved to them the error of their ways, silencing them at least temporarily, and provoking their anger even more.

Today I want you to consider something with me. We can be all three characters from this story at different times. Sometimes we're the woman, caught in our sin, at Jesus' feet looking for mercy. "Go, and sin no more" is one of the most powerful phrases you will read in this book, and I suggest you take it to heart.

Other times we are like Jesus in this story, helping to release people from condemnation in the midst of their mess. We need to know that the people we encounter are struggling with all sorts of ugly things. In fact, there is stuff out there that people have done that could make you vomit, but when you're standing there talking to someone, you must look at them through the eyes of Jesus. Compassion will fill your heart as you call them to live a holy life.

More often than not, we all unfortunately get stuck in the spot of the religious leaders, getting upset over man-made rules that have little or nothing to do with what Christ taught. We are often the ones trying to trap Jesus, because we don't like what He said or the way He said it, so we write it off as if He meant something else. Or we were taught some off-the-wall version of what Jesus said that isn't backed up by any translation of the Bible, but because it sounds great and serves our agendas, we love it.

We like to sit and pick at people, telling them all the things they need to change about their lives, or even more commonly, we tell everyone but that person all the things we see wrong. Gossip and slander fill the church in America, as most people sit back idling, doing nothing except maybe attending a meeting once a week, but they're expert fault-finders.

Which of the three characters in the story are you today? Are you the sinner needing to repent and receive forgiveness? Are you the man of God, extending mercy? Are you the Pharisee trying to figure out how to destroy someone else's ministry because you're full of jealousy and hatred? If the last one is you, you also need to repent. Let's all ask the Lord, what is inside of me that I need to repent for? What is inside of me that I need to hand over to Jesus?

Jesus' instructions to the woman are the same to all of us, "Go and sin no more."

DAY 11
MARSHFIELD, WI

PLAYING IN THE RAIN

Believe it or not, there is a third part to the story from the last two days. They literally all took place within the same 24 hours.

When we got back to the church after visiting the magic store, you may remember that I had been asked to pray with this lady during the service. At the very end of the session, she said the Lord had given her permission to play. She told us about how when she was a kid, she was never able to play because she was responsible for taking care of her siblings. One time when she was young, she had tried to swing on some swings and her dad beat her for it. But that night the Lord released her to play.

When she said that, I asked her, "So, do you want to play?"

She looked at me like she was confused and asked, "Right now?"

"The Lord gave you permission to play, so we should play," I responded.

My mind was racing. Whose kids were here? My kids were at home, and most of the other missionaries' kids were gone for the week, so who could we get to play with us? Christian! He has kids! I asked the lady if she knew if there was a park nearby, and she said that there was one about a half mile down the road.

I jumped up and said, "Okay. Hold on."

Christian was outside when I found him. "Hey Christian, can I borrow your kids?" I asked.

"They went home," he said in his strong German accent.

"Hmm, who could play with us…?" I thought.

Next to Christian was this amazing 13-year-old boy and his dad. I asked the kid, "Hey man! You want to go to the park and play?"

He was confused and asked why.

I said, "Look, we prayed with this lady and the Lord gave her permission to play, so we're trying to find someone who could play with us at the park. You want to join us?"

His dad was behind him and he said, "It's going to rain. There's lightning. Are you sure this is a good idea?"

I said, "The Lord gave her permission to play, and I really think we need to do it now. Rain or not."

"We're in!" the father said.

Christian and Garrett overheard the whole thing and wanted to come too. He has a Toyota Sienna which can fit eight or so people in it. I grabbed our crew and eight of us went to the playground at a school about half a mile from the host church.

It was about 10:30 at night, and we were running, and laughing, and carrying on at the park. The teenager was going down the slides so he could dry them off a bit for the woman. There was lightning, and it had really started to rain, but you could feel the joy in the air. The freedom she was experiencing was incredible to be a part of. She smiled so big, and told us that were the craziest people she'd ever met.

"That very well may be true," I thought to myself.

While we were playing, we heard some additional laughing and carrying on. It turns out three ladies heard us having fun from across the street and decided to join us. Apparently it's a thing now, to play at the school playground late at night in a thunderstorm.

Because our group was so large, we split up and some of us stayed to play and the rest of us went to see how we could minister to these ladies. I believe that the Lord brought them. Why else in the world would they have been out there? As we approached, there was a group of people across the street screaming for them and one of the three started to leave. We quickly asked her how we could pray for her and she responded with "good health."

The closer we got and the more we could understand them, and smell them, we could tell that they were all pretty wasted. I prayed a fast prayer for the girl that was leaving and we asked the other two how we could pray for them. One of them was pregnant, so we were able to bless her pregnancy. Garrett had something from the Lord that he felt he needed to release over them, so he did that. Then we offered them wristbands and they excitedly accepted them.

By this time the rain was getting pretty thick, and I didn't want to ruin the Bibles by having them get wet, so we asked if they would be willing to stand under the awning outside their house. Our whole crew walked over there, and the people that were inside partying were livid. They started screaming all kinds of craziness because they didn't want us to come into their house. We hadn't been planning to, but the more we tried to explain, the weirder everything got.

There was a large pine tree close by, so we decided to go stand underneath it. Garrett had a super cool military flashlight on him, so we could provide enough light for both ladies to be able to read through the verses. There we were, eight people from Revive, all standing in the rain under a pine tree with a flashlight, sharing the gospel with two women.

When we asked what would be in the way of them accepting Christ, one of the girls had an issue. We prayed with her and counseled her, and she decided that nothing was in the way and that she wanted to receive Jesus right then. They wanted to repeat after one of us, and Christian led them in a sinner's prayer. Both of them were born again that night, all because a woman who was given permission to play was willing to act like an idiot at a playground, super late at night, leading us to be there at the same time these two women were. That's amazing!

There is a story in the Bible of this crazy amazing guy named Phillip. When we are first introduced to him in Acts 6, he's being voted in to help take care of the distribution of food, so that the

Apostles can focus on teaching and other cool stuff. But persecution hits and the next time we see him, he's preaching the gospel and tons of people are getting saved and baptized because they believed the message.

> The Holy Spirit said to Philip, "Go over and walk along beside the carriage."
> Philip ran over and heard the man reading from the prophet Isaiah. Philip asked, "Do you understand what you are reading?" (Acts 8:29-30)

Philip ends up being able to explain the prophecy this guy was reading, which was about Jesus, and "beginning with this same scripture, Philip told him the Good News about Jesus" (v. 35). The guy, who was a eunuch, gets saved and sees a river nearby, so Philip baptized him too.

The reason that Philip was able to lead the eunuch to Jesus was because he was willing to respond to the Holy Spirit's instructions. He could have decided to wait a day, but that man wouldn't have been there. Some people call this a divine appointment. Call it whatever you want, but there is no way Philip could have known to go right there, at that moment, to run up to some guy's chariot/carriage, so that he could ask a eunuch about the book he's reading, unless it was divine. THAT IS CRAZY. You couldn't make up that kind of timing.

God took a man who knew the answers to the eunuch's questions and put them together even though on their own they never would have run into each other. Philip was available and willing to be used, so God used him.

Here's the deal. Some of are so used to tuning out the Lord because we think what we've been asked to do sounds stupid, or crazy, or it'll never work, and yet there is a huge chance that you are missing a divine appointment where you could have changed the course of history in someone's life.

Let's be available for the Lord to do stuff in us right away. Let's be willing to play in the rain so that someone can experience freedom in Christ. Even if we're in a desert, and it's hot, and we don't want to be around people, let's be willing enough that if God says to run, we will.

There are so many times where God has set everything up so perfectly that those looking in know that I am too much of a dork-wad to be able to set all that up myself. God be glorified, when people obey the Holy Spirit. God be praised, when people are willing to step out of their norms so that they can teach someone a difficult passage of scripture.

Today let's be open to anything the Holy Spirit puts in front of us. Today is the day to step out in faith and trust the Father. Listen for His voice, and be willing to act on what you're told.

DAY 12
TERRE HAUTE, IN

JESUS IS ALWAYS WITH YOU

My team had been specifically asked to go to a neighborhood that the crew in Terre Haute had been trying to reach for a while. My friend Art, his wife, their daughter, and I were all on a team together. We had decided to go to the playground so that their daughter could play and it seemed like there were quite a few people out and about in that neighborhood so we figured we would be able to talk with someone there.

As we approached the playground, there were some teenagers doing something called parkour. It is an extreme sports type thing, where you have to jump off and over and around things like park benches and swing sets. We asked them to show us their coolest moves, and they were glad to oblige. They told us the name for each of the moves as they did them.

As they finished, we began to talk about all sorts of things. They told us their ages were 17, 15, and 14 and that their favorite subject was history. My favorite class in school was history too, so I asked them about their favorite time periods. They each said a different time, but all when tons of people died. The seventeen-year-old said that his favorite time in history was the Holocaust. (I clarified to make sure he didn't mean WWII in general. His favorite really was the Holocaust.)

He told me that he loved reading about Hitler, because he was intriguing. He thought it was crazy that Hitler would murder so many Jews when he was one himself. (This is what this guy said. I am by no means telling you this as a fact.) As he continued to talk about Hitler and how he was Jewish, I had an idea.

I asked, "Hey, Jesus was a Jew, what do you think about Him?"

He told me that he's an atheist and had done a lot of reading on religion. He recognized that Jesus had been a real person at one point in time, but wasn't convinced that He was God. The other two boys had similar views, but one said he was more agnostic, in that he really just didn't know for sure. They all agreed though that there was a real guy at one point in history named Jesus, and that He did die on a cross.

At this I asked them if it would be okay if Art and I told them what WE thought about Jesus. They agreed and so we passed out wristbands and Bibles. I told them that if at any point in time this got weird or uncomfortable to let me know and we'd stop. They agreed to let us proceed.

We went through all the colors, and on the green verse I told them, "It says that you have to believe in your heart that Jesus was raised from the dead. Now, that's pretty crazy, don't you think?" They all agreed. "How many of you know someone who has been raised from the dead?"

They all said, "We were."

This shocked me! "What!" I said. "What do you mean you were all raised from the dead?"

They each told us about how they had died and then came back to life, and two of them said they had had "out of body experiences."

I said, "Okay, tell me about it."

And so the atheist started to tell me about how he died, came out of his body, and watched as the fireman did CPR on his body, and then when his body came back to life, he was sucked back in.

I felt the Lord prompt me to do something I had never done before. I said, "Do me a favor. Close your eyes."

He did. I promised him that I wouldn't touch him or do anything weird, and I wouldn't even move from where I was standing.

I said, "Now do me another favor. Ask Jesus, 'Where were you when the fireman was bringing me back to life?'"

Out loud, he repeated the question with his eyes closed. Right after he prayed those words, his face changed. He looked up at me, his eyes really big in disbelief.

I asked, "Well, where was He?"

"He was behind the fireman!"

"Well, what was He doing?"

"His hand was out."

"Was it His right hand or His left hand?"

"It was His right hand."

"Well, what does that mean?"

He said he didn't know. I said, "Do you think it means come here?"

"Yeah!" He said, and his eyes got even bigger.

"Do you think He was trying to say 'Come to me now,' like He wants you to die and go be with Him?"

"No."

"Do you think He was trying to say 'Come follow me?'"

"YEAH!" And somehow his eyes got even bigger again!

I told him, "That is why I am here man, because you didn't listen to Him when He called you. He sent me here today to call you to come follow Him."

The atheist sat there in disbelief. At that point I said to all of them, "Who wants this gift that we've been talking to you about?"

Some of you reading this may not know anything about me, but my voice is pretty loud, and when I share the gospel I can unknowingly talk louder than normal. (Sorry in advance. My intentions aren't to blow your eardrums.)

Five more boys, of all different ages, had heard me say "gift" and ran up wanting wristbands and Bibles. We tried to explain to them that Jesus was the gift that we were offering. They decided to repeat after us in a prayer, so Art lead all eight of those young men in a prayer of repentance and confessing Christ as their Lord. Everyone was so happy. The agnostic guy said his dad was going to be really excited, because he'd been praying for him, and he couldn't wait to tell him.

The atheist told me as we were walking away, "Man, I have been wrestling with this stuff for so long, and right now I have so much clarity."

When I think about this story, what really changed everything was the moment when the no-longer-atheist saw Jesus. In Mark, we see a similar comparison.

> After Jesus rose from the dead early on Sunday morning, the first person who saw Him was Mary Magdalene, the woman from whom He had cast out seven demons. She went to the disciples, who were grieving and weeping, and told them what had happened. But when she told them that Jesus was alive and she had seen Him, they didn't believe her. (Mark 16:9-11)

According to each of the gospels Mary had already been to the tomb, and John 20 describes how she'd led the disciples on an emotional roller coaster because she'd told them the first time she went to the tomb that Jesus' body had been stolen. This caused Peter and John to get up and race to the tomb to find no body. Ultimately what changed in Mary was that she encountered Jesus. She had initially been told that Jesus was alive by the angels she found in the tomb, and yet she didn't believe them.

Whenever you go out to pray for someone or to love on someone, your goal must be this: they need to encounter the living Jesus. He IS alive. Jesus Christ is not dead. That is what makes our green verses, Romans 10:9-10, so amazing to me. You have to be willing to say that you believe in your heart that a man named Jesus died on a cross because He loved you and me, that He rose from the dead on the third day, and that He never re-died, but ascended to the Father and is seated there now on His right side, where He's interceding for each of us.

We need the lost to encounter a living, breathing Jesus. It is our job to make the introduction. When you show love to someone, you can know that that person is going to experience Jesus, at least a little bit, because John tells us that "God is love" (1 John 4:16). That means Jesus is also love.

Today, while you're reading this story, I pray that you're encountering Jesus even now. Maybe it's been a while for you, and you're running dry. Before you leave for work, or go to bed, or whatever is next in your day, go to your closet, get on your knees, close your eyes, and get with Jesus.

If you don't know what to say or where to start, just say this, "Here I am Jesus to be with you. What would you like to tell me?" If you want to have your Bible with you while you do it, great! There isn't a formula to this. The idea is to be with Jesus. Ask Him to reveal who you need to share the gospel with. Then go and tell that person, just like Mary did. "I have seen the Lord!" (John 20:18). You don't have to use those words verbatim, but say something, anything. The lost need to be found. Someone today needs you to share the good news with them. Don't delay.

DAY 13
TUPELO, MS

INAPPROPRIATE U-TURN

A group of us from northern Indiana who had been radically changed by what God had been doing in our lives through Revive had heard they were going to be in Tupelo, Mississippi so we decided to go help. As we were leaving to go back to Indiana, we stopped at a gas station to get gas and some of us went inside to grab snacks.

When I got back into the van, our driver Roger said, "Hey, do you see that lady over there?"

To the left of the vehicle there was a lady standing outside of her car with a young child sitting on the cement barrier. "I feel like I should talk to them... What do you think?"

"I don't know man... Why don't you try it?"

"No, no... It's just my flesh." Roger said.

"Man, if you have the desire to talk to them, why don't you just try it and see? You can take your wife with you that way it's not super weird," I said as another couple of people got into the van.

"What's going on?" a guy named Ryan asked.

"Oh, Roger is trying to decide if he should talk to that lady over there, the one with her kid," I said pointing to her. (I was in the back of the van, which had tinted windows, so she didn't see me point.)

"Why don't you try it?" Ryan asked.

"No, no, no," Roger said, "it's just my flesh."

The rest of our crew got in the car and Roger started to pull away, as he watched the lady and her son.

"Just get out and try it," we kept telling Roger.

"No, guys, I think it's just my flesh." And Roger pulled away from the gas station.

"You probably just messed up a divine appointment, man!" we all told him.

"You're right!" Roger said. "I should at least try it!"

We had just pulled onto the on-ramp to get on the highway, and Roger cranked the wheel to do a U-turn. We drove back to the gas station, and he and his wife Jo went to get out of the van when the lady and her son got into their car and pulled away!

"Oh no!" we all said, bummed that we missed our chance.

In the back seat Ryan prayed, "Lord, if we are supposed to talk to them, make them turn around!"

We all watched as their car headed to the on-ramp. Then all of a sudden, their vehicle pulls onto the on-ramp and then U-turns, just like we did! They came back toward the gas station, but pulled into a empty driveway across the street.

"NOW YOU HAVE TO DO IT!" we told Roger.

Roger and Jo got out of the car, while we stayed and prayed for them. We watched as they gave them both a Bible and band and went through the colors. We tried to be sneaky in the van, rolling the windows down to listen, but the sounds from the highway were so loud that we couldn't hear anything. Eventually Roger and Jo came back, smiling.

"What happened?" we asked Roger.

"The first thing we asked them," Roger began, "was why in the world they turned around. They told us that they needed to stretch their legs!"

"No way!" we all said. They had just been doing that the entire time we were at the gas station earlier.

"They are also Jewish," Roger said. "We were able to share the gospel with them and they thanked us for doing so."

We were all thrilled. Even though nobody was saved from it, we believe that what happened will be a monument in their life. They will be able to look back and see the first time the gospel was shared with them, and how much Jesus really cares for His people.

My friend came up with a skit that we use to teach people what NOT to do in an encounter. Really, it's genius, and super funny, and sad. We pretend we are out on a team to share the gospel, and we pray and ask God to show us who to talk to and then when He does, and we see that person, we talk ourselves out of talking to them. For example, we prayed and a few pretended to hear from the Lord about a guy with a beard, and then a guy with a beard comes walking by us and we're like, "Well I think it was more of an 'Abraham Lincoln' beard, not a 'lumberjack' beard."

The truth is that this exact thing happens everywhere we go. It tends to happen more for people who are introverted or aren't as seasoned with talking to new people, but it happens to everyone. If I am honest, there are feelings of fear before every encounter I have. The difference is, I don't let the feelings stop me. It requires me to dig deep, and put my trust in Jesus instead of myself.

There was a day when I relied on my humor and my charm to get me through encounters, and let's just say that not many people got saved. The truth is though that a lot of people are crippled with fear to talk to a stranger, or anyone, about Jesus because we have been taught that you don't talk about controversial topics, you avoid debate and conflict.

By no means am I saying you should argue and debate, but I am saying that you CAN talk about Jesus, and people want to hear about Him even though we think they don't. It's a lie that we believe. We think that the proper protocol is to wait for them to ask us about it. I am all for being wise, and cautious, and gentle, but I also know you can talk about Jesus and people will respond. Sometimes they get angry, sure, but not most of the time.

Recently I was doing a study on fear, and I discovered that in scripture, the only thing you have permission to fear is the Lord, yet most of us fear what people will say or won't say. We fear rejection and disappointment and failure. We fear talking with someone who knows more than us, or interacting with a smelly guy for two hours.

2 Timothy 1:7 says this, "For God has not given us a spirit of fear and timidity, but of power, love, and self-discipline." One thing that stood out to me when I checked the original Greek word, was that another word that could be used instead of "fear" or "timidity" is "cowardice." You have not been given a spirit of cowardice, but of power, love, and self-discipline.

Think about this. Now every time you don't talk to your lost coworker about Jesus, even though you feel a tug when you see him, just because you don't want to lose your job or offend someone, that is timidity, fear, or cowardice. I grew up watching John Wayne movies, and he would call people "yeller" or "yeller-livered" for being a coward.

You have been given a spirit of power, don't be afraid! The One on your team is way bigger and scarier than anything you can come up against. You have been given a spirit of love. No matter what you run into out there, there is never someone who cannot be loved. Love compels us to rise and act instead of cower in the corner. You have also been given self-discipline. This means that when you're afraid, your feelings don't have to dictate your actions.

Today ask the Lord if you have been walking in fear. Are there people with whom you have talked yourself out of sharing the gospel? When the Lord exposes your insides, repent. Then go and talk to those people you haven't shared with yet.

DAY 14
CHAMPAIGN CO, OH

HANGING OUT WITH TROUBLE

My team was sent to a tiny town in the middle of nowhere, with a population less than one hundred. All they had was a church and a pizza place! We were sent to the church to pray before going throughout the town to see who we could pray for.

As we turned the corner to pull onto the church's road, we saw a young man walking by our car in the grass on the side of the road. I immediately wanted to talk to him, but my team was really excited to get to the church and pray. Part of me was bummed, because I didn't want to miss him, but I felt that it was necessary for the sake of my team to keep going.

I prayed, "Lord, if you want me to talk to him, make him come back to us." Sometimes people pray this so they don't have to interact with someone, but that was by no means my heart. When we arrived at the church nobody was there, and my team decided to do a prayer walk around the property, which again made my heart sink. How would I ever get to that young man?

My daughter Mercy came with us as we prayer-walked around the church grounds. It's a pretty large property, and most of it is a graveyard. We prayed that the congregation would be more alive than their property. As we were coming back around to the front, I saw that same young man, and he was walking toward the church! Immediately I knew, the time was now.

The church had a small play set and Mercy went to play on it while he approached. He walked right up to the church and so we struck up a conversation. As it turned out, the young man comes to this particular church all the time so that he doesn't have to stay at home. He had left a dvd player and a sweater on the steps.

As we started interacting with this young man, we found out that one of the ladies on my team used to be his teacher. It had been a few years and he had grown so much that she didn't recognize him at all. He explained to us that his home life was pretty rough and it's easier to be out of the house than at home.

At that point a lady pulled into the church parking lot, and one of our team members walked over to engage her. She warned us not to mess with that young man, because he's nothing but trouble.

After we talked with him for a while, we asked if there was anything we could pray for him about, and he didn't really know. I asked if he'd ever had anyone ask him that before and he said no. He let us pray a general blessing over his life. I gave him the wristband and asked if he'd like to know what the colors mean. He said, "Not really."

"DENIED," was all I could think. My flesh screamed that we were done, and needed to move on. My faith had gone right out the window. Two of us had turned to leave when the teacher asked him another question. He had started to tell us before how incredibly fast he was. She challenged him to show us.

"You say you are pretty fast, but you could be lying," we told him. So he decided to prove it.

His house was just down the street, and he told us that he would skateboard back home and run back to us as fast as he could. There was a hill on down the street and he would scream really loudly before he took off, that way we could time how long it took. It was a quarter mile from the church to his house. (We didn't take the time to verify it.)

As he rode off on his skateboard, the teacher started to explain to us that she knew the young man's family really well. She could guarantee that nobody had ever given him any kind of encouragement. His mom had a string of men in and out of the house, and they were all abusive. Drugs and other substance abuses were also common. At one point while we had been talking to him, he told us about how his dad was in jail because he had tried to abort him with a kitchen knife.

We waited for him to come running over the hill and tried to see where he'd gone and how far it really was. All of a sudden there it was, a shout! I started the timer on my phone and sure enough, he came sprinting over the hill. We cheered as loudly as we could for him, and when he got to us, we cheered some more! His time was fifty seconds (if it really was a quarter mile, that would be super fast.)

He was really out of breath. As we told him how great he was, he just smiled and paced back and forth, gloating a little. I asked if he had ever considered running cross country. He responded that he was thinking about running track. We encouraged him to join the team, since he would be a senior in high school that year. I said that if he worked hard at it, he might be able to get a scholarship to a college and be a famous runner someday. (I readily admit I am by no means a expert on fast people, but he needed to hear that someone believed in him, and I do.)

As he was still trying to catch his breath, it reminded me of how our team sometimes trains on the word "demonstrate" because our red verse uses that word. I said to him, "You know, what you did for us was a demonstration of how fast you are, right?"

He agreed that it was, so I kept going. "This is super crazy, but God demonstrates His love for us in a similar way that you just demonstrated how incredibly fast you are."

He wanted to know more, so I showed him our Bible, turned to the red tab, and said, "Look, this verse talks about a demonstration. In this demonstration, God shows us how much he loves us."

We ended up going through the whole wristband with him and this young man was born again. I was so thankful that my teammate didn't give up on him. Honestly, this is part of why it's so important to go out with at least one other person. Jesus sent his disciples out in twos. They have something to offer that you don't have.

This young man told us that he'd never heard the gospel before and he committed to being discipled by the pastor of that church, who one of my team members knew personally.

Matthew 8:3 says, "Jesus reached out and touched him. 'I am willing,' he said. 'Be healed!' And instantly the leprosy disappeared." Now, I know my story isn't about a man with leprosy, but is about a young man that nobody wanted to be around. The lady from town knew him and didn't want to be around him in the same way nobody would have wanted to be around the guy with leprosy. Lepers were required to stay out of the town in a separate colony so they didn't spread their disease around.

What I love about this story is that Jesus physically touches the guy that has a disease transferred through skin contact. Jesus wasn't afraid to touch the man. Why? I believe it is because He knew who He was, and He knew the power in Him was greater than the leprosy. He took the power that He had, and applied it to the leper's situation causing his body to be healed.

In our case, we took the love inside of us and applied the power of the gospel to a young man who was riddled with sin. We spoke into his life and cheered for him when nobody wanted anything to do with him.

Today, as you read this story, ask the Lord to show you someone like this. Who do I need to go to today? Maybe this will require you to drive to the shady side of town. Maybe this will require you to stop at the seedy motel and pray for that lady that stands on the side-walk. Whatever the Lord puts on your heart to do, respond to that in obedience.

Don't walk in fear of whatever they have. The power that is inside of you is greater than anything you face. The God that spoke the universe into being and raised Jesus from the dead lives inside you. Walk it out.

DAY 15
DARKE COUNTY, OH

JOHN WAYNE

Sometimes I feel like I am pretty awful at this. There are times when I go out to share the gospel, and it really doesn't seem to go well. You just have to keep praying and trust that the Lord knows what He's doing.

This particular day my team felt led to go to a trailer park. As it turns out, there was one about a quarter of a mile from the host church. When my team pulled in, right away I saw a man sitting under an awning so we drove up the road a little, pulled over, and my buddy Justin and I got out. We approached the man cautiously, trying not to draw attention to the fact we had just parked across the street.

I greeted the man from the road, "Nice day, isn't it!"

"Yeah it is," the man replied, "What do you want?"

It really drives me nuts when people ask me that, because I like to work my way into why we're there and not just come out with it, but when it happens I just respond with the truth.

"We're with reviveOhio and are going throughout the community trying to see how we can pray for people," I told him. "Is there anything we could pray with you about?"

"No," he said, "I don't like prayer."

I told him, "I just so happen to be really good at talking about other things as well, like John Wayne."

"John WAYNE!" he said as he stood from his chair. "I have every John Wayne movie ever made!"

"WOW!" I said, as Justin and I started to cross his yard to get closer to him.

"What's your favorite John Wayne movie?" he asked me.

"Well, I'd have to say *True Grit* right now, but I also really like *Big Jake.*"

The man began to quote large portions of *True Grit*. He sat back down and I kneeled beside him, smiling as he quoted the movie.

"I have every John Wayne movie ever made," he said a second time, "on both DVD and VHS!"

"WOW!" I said again. "Where do you keep them? You have a pretty small house."

He laughed and we talked more about John Wayne movies.

After a while he finally said, "You know, my back has been hurting for a long time, I guess you could pray for my back?"

"We would love to," I said. "Would it be okay if I put my hand on your back where the pain is?"

"If it makes you happy," the man said.

I put my hand on his back and commanded it to come into alignment and the pain to be gone in Jesus' name. I asked the man how he felt, and he said he couldn't really tell a difference while he was sitting. So he stood up to test his back and said, "Wow! IT IS BETTER!"

He was shocked that the prayer worked. We asked him if he'd like a wristband to remind him that we prayed. He happily took the wristband and asked what the colors represent. We gave him a Bible and walked him through the scriptures. He put his trust in Jesus and was born again!

Jesus also said, "The Kingdom of God is like a farmer who scatters seed on the ground. Night and day, while he's asleep or awake, the seed sprouts and grows, but he does not understand how it happens. The earth produces the crops on its own. First a leaf blade pushes through, then the heads of wheat are formed, and finally the grain ripens. And as soon as the grain is ready, the farmer comes and harvests it with a sickle, for the harvest time has come." (Mark 4:26-29)

One of the things that I have learned in my time with Revive is that not everyone is ready to be harvested. Sometimes the Lord will tell you in advance if they're ready or not, but other times you just have to follow through, keep asking questions, and present the gospel. Sometimes you are the sower, and other times you are the harvester. Rarely are you both.

It has been a process for me to learn to be okay with just sowing the seed. Our culture today tends to measure worth by performance, how much money you have, and your family line. We are all battling a mindset that says, "If you aren't working your tail off, you aren't worth much." If you have low numbers you're looked down upon.

I have to recognize the reality that sometimes my job is to sow and other times it is to harvest, but either way I cannot grow that seed. The Lord has to do that. As much as I would love to have the ability to make someone ready to be saved, that is out of my hands.

Notice too that the plant doesn't necessarily "sprout" overnight. It could if God wanted it to, because He is powerful enough, but for most people it's a process. I love that it says that whether the farmer is "asleep or awake...the earth produces the crop on its own." This takes the pressure off of having to perform. It's not about you being awesome at sharing the gospel, it's just about you being faithful to sow and, when you see the fruit is ripe, pick it.

Today as you spend time in prayer, ask the Lord if you've been trying to make seed grow. Maybe you need to repent for trying to do a job that isn't yours. Maybe you need to ask the Lord where you should sow, and take along your sickle just in case there's fruit ready. Maybe you're reading this and realizing that you haven't been faithful to harvest or sow, and you've been waiting for your pastor to do it. Today is your day. Repent and get to work. Go sow your seeds in Jesus' name and reap the harvest that is produced. "The harvest time has come." There are people ready to be picked. Let's get to work.

DAY 16
DARKE COUNTY, OH

LAWN MOWER VS. SEED SOWER

During a Revive outreach week, we have a time of testimonies while we eat lunch. My friend Kyle came up to me one day as I was getting ready to head to the lunch church and said, "Hey man, last night I had a dream where I saw signs with the names of the streets at an intersection. I just looked it up and it's right up the street from the church. Would you want to go with me?"

"Absolutely!" I said.

So we walked from the lunch church to the intersection from Kyle's dream. When we arrived there were two guys mowing a yard, but other than that there wasn't anyone out and about. We decided not to interrupt their work, so instead we walked around to see what we could find. We made a pretty large circle and prayed for a few people, but for the most part nobody was out.

As we approached the intersection again, we saw that the guys were finishing up. I prayed out loud, "Lord, if we are supposed to talk to those guys, let them be finished when we arrive."

Literally as we got to the truck, they had just finished loading the equipment and were getting ready to leave. We told them about Kyle's dream from the night before about this exact intersection, then we googled the address and it just happened to be right up the road from where we were going. We recognized that we might be a little strange, but we didn't believe it was an accident that we were there.

They agreed that we were strange, as they nodded their heads and smiled, and we asked how we could pray. They gave us super common answers like world peace and a good business year. We prayed for them and gave them wristbands.

They let us explain the scriptures and, as it turned out, the older man was already saved and had been coming to the evening services for reviveOHIO, but his son was not. He flat out told us he wasn't ready. Kyle began to speak into him. He nodded his head to everything Kyle said as if to say, "Yeah, that's right."

Then the Lord gave me a word for him. As I released it, I felt as if everything I said just fell flat. I was so discouraged. It made me never want to try doing that again.

The next day, I was at the lunch location watching my kids in the playroom when Kyle came up to me and said, "You won't believe who I just ran into!"

"WHO?" I asked.

"That young man from yesterday that we prayed for but didn't want Jesus. He is across the street right now!"

"What!"

"I didn't see him until he grabbed me and said that he really appreciated us sharing with him yesterday. He said that we were right on. In fact he said, 'That other guy that was with you…everything he shared with me was in my dream the night before I met you guys.'"

I just stood there staring for a minute because I was so shocked!

"What! NO WAY!" I said. "That's amazing! Here I was thinking that I was just way off base!"

"Nope!" Kyle said. "He actually thanked us for sharing and he said he is close to getting saved, but he's just not ready yet."

In the story you just read, it bothered me that I felt like I was speaking from the Lord, but it didn't seem like it was hitting home for the guy. He just looked unfazed. I was so intimidated, especially because I knew he didn't want to get saved.

There are a lot of people out there that want an exact word-for-word plan before they share the gospel. Often times this is because they are used to having to debate, so they want to practice what they are going to say beforehand. "Well…if they say this…then I will say this…" You don't have to do that. Why? Because when you're standing there in obedience, the Holy Spirit is going to speak the right words through you.

Sure, it will be scary. Even if your life is not being threatened, it can be scary. How much more scary is it to disobey the Lord! I would rather speak out of the bad pizza I had yesterday and know that I tried, than to never have said anything at all and missed a moment that heaven could have touched someone. If I feel the prompting of the Spirit, I need to not quench it, but to respond with obedience. This is what it means when you say "Jesus is Lord." You are not in charge of your own life anymore.

You may not always be able to have a confirmation like I did the next day, saying that you were spot on. The way that you get the confidence to speak through the Spirit is by trying it. Take the risk of looking like a fool. Stop holding onto your dignity and pride, and allow the Lord to work through you.

1 Peter 5:6 says, "So humble yourselves under the mighty power of God, and at the right time He will lift you up in honor." We really should stop caring so much about always being right and start caring about obedience. If we humble ourselves, God is going to lift us up at the right time. We can't do it ourselves.

No more can we worry about if we look sexy or cool, or how people will receive us. We need to worry about obeying the voice of God, and when He says to speak, SPEAK. Even if you don't know what to say in advance, that's okay. Stop allowing fear to control your life. It's not yours to control anymore, remember?

> When you are arrested, don't worry about how to respond or what to say. God will give you the right words at the right time. For it is not you who will be speaking—it will be the Spirit of your Father speaking through you. (Matt. 10:19-20)

I could be wrong, but when I read this verse in context, this is what I get out of it. There will be times when you'll be in stressful situations, but instead of worrying, trust God. He will give you the words to say. In fact the Lord says that the Holy Spirit, His Spirit, will be speaking through you. I don't think this only applies to being arrested.

Anytime you need to speak, but especially when you're listening to the Spirit, don't worry about what to say. If God is going to show up and speak through us in those moments when our lives are on the line, why wouldn't He do the same when we're sharing the gospel?

John 14:26 says that the Holy Spirit "will teach you everything and will remind you of everything I have told you." So we know that when the pressure is on, the Holy Spirit can and will bring to mind that which Christ has already put in our hearts, through the spiritual discipline of studying the Word of God. The Spirit can even speak things through those who have never read or studied, if they will allow it.

In my story earlier, you saw an example where I had spoken something that the man had experienced the night before in a dream. I believe that sometimes the Lord tells you things before you say them, but then other times it's like He just asks you to open your mouth and He'll speak through you.

In Luke 6 we see a story where the religious leaders of the day were trying to catch Jesus working on the Sabbath. Jesus was teaching at the local synagogue, and a guy that needed healing was there.

> But Jesus knew their thoughts. He said to the man with the deformed hand, "Come and stand in front of everyone." So the man came forward. (Luke 6:8)

As the man stood there in front of everyone, Jesus asked if it was okay to heal people on the Sabbath, which of course disgusted the religious leaders, and Jesus healed the guy anyway.

The part that I would like to focus on is that "Jesus knew their thoughts." How could any of us know anyone's thoughts without them telling us? Words of knowledge. We have said before that the Holy Spirit will sometimes tell you things about someone that is so intimate they haven't told anyone, and then they will know that God is real because of it.

> At this, the enemies of Jesus were wild with rage and began
> to discuss what to do with Him. (Luke 6:11)

Sometimes when you are operating through the Holy Spirit, people won't be all that thrilled with you. In Jesus' case, upsetting the religious provoked them to want to murder Him at a later time. Don't be surprised if people aren't always excited that you told them one of their own secrets. However, I want to encourage you that even if people are upset with you, or provoked to anger (as long as you weren't being a jerk about it) that doesn't mean that you shouldn't have done it. Sometimes it's necessary for the big picture of what God is doing. Sometimes it's to refine you.

Here's some practical advice for you. If you're out and about and you know the Lord gave you something that could be a word of knowledge, ask yourself some quick questions. First, is this something that could be considered intimate and should be shared more privately, out of courtesy for the other person?

Second, ask yourself how best to deliver it. Have some humility in your approach. People are really burned out by the "God said" stuff. Whether you're right or wrong, it may not matter because your gift was wrapped in a way that made it appear like a bomb, so they didn't open it. Wrap it up nice, so when it's delivered they'll receive it well.

Finally, ask yourself if what God showed you needs to be shared at all. I believe that at times God shows you something about what's going on with a person, not so you can tell them about it, but so that you can pray for them.

There was a time in Chicago where the group that I was with spoke mostly Spanish. Even though I have Mexican heritage, I can only say a few phrases in Spanish. (I am working on it.) We had been at a corner store talking to a group of guys who all of a sudden left the store, got in their cars, and drove off. One of the ladies in my group started wailing while we stood on the corner. I was confused. The rest of our group started to cry and call out to the Lord (I did understand that).

After a while, things calmed down and we started to walk away. The only girl with us that spoke any English told me about how the lady who first started to cry had seen a vision of those young men, heading off to kill a young man. So they all stopped to pray that God would intervene.

I had contemplated calling the police, but I didn't know how well "my friend who speaks a different language than me said she saw a vision of these guys committing a murder" would go. So I prayed that the Lord would handle it.

Now, if what they saw was true, which I believe it was, then this would actually be a prophetic vision. But the question we'd ask ourselves is the same. Is this something I need to do something about? Or am I supposed to take this to the Lord in prayer? Not everything needs to be spoken. The Lord will give you wisdom and discernment on this matter if you ask.

Today ask the Lord to speak through you at some point. Allow yourself, at work or maybe in your neighborhood, to stand before someone without an agenda or a rehearsed message, and let the Holy Spirit speak through you. You can do it. You need to do it. They need you to do it.

DAY 17
BEMIDJI, MN

LET THE CHILDREN COME TO ME

I wasn't planning to share this story, but while I was praying, the Lord kept bringing it to my mind. So... here it is.

One Sunday evening reviveMinnesota decided to have a hog roast and invite the community. Over five hundred people showed up that day and everything was a bit crazy. I was trying to keep my kids from snatching extra cookies AND do my job.

One of our team members came to me and said, "There's a young man who is incredibly shy, and his mom would like you to pray with him."

So I went over to him. He was sitting in the tent and eating his food while the band was practicing. His mom and I interacted for a bit, and I asked him if he would be willing to sit outside the tent so that maybe we could hear each other better. He was so soft spoken, I couldn't really tell if he was saying yes or no, especially because he would not look at me. As soon as I sat next to him, he put his head down.

He finally nodded, so I set up some chairs outside the tent and we sat where he could see his mom and his mom could see us, that way nobody could accuse me of doing anything weird. (In general I try not to be one-on-one with kids that aren't my own. It presents too many problems. But since there were hundreds of people who could see us, I figured it would be okay.)

I asked him how I could pray for him, and he didn't have an answer. I asked him if he knew his dad, and he said, "Sort of."

"Is it okay if I pray for your relationship with your dad?"

He nodded. I asked him if I could put my hand on his shoulder and he nodded again.

My heart went out to this young man. It was really obvious that he had never had a male figure pour into him. He had shame and insecurity all over him, and it was all I could do not to cry. I thanked the Father for being a good father, and afterwards I explained why I had prayed that. He doesn't leave us or forsake us. Our heavenly Father is there for us when we need it, and He loves us deeply. The young man seemed to be listening.

I asked him if he would like to know his heavenly Father. And he said yes. I gave him a wristband and gently walked him through the scriptures. He read all of them out loud, very timidly. The entire time I talked with him, he didn't look up. I wished that I knew what was going on in his mind.

I told him that if he accepted Jesus into his heart, he would be able to know his heavenly Father because Jesus said, "Anyone who has seen me has seen the Father!" (John 14:9). He prayed a prayer asking Jesus to forgive him of his sins and to come into his heart. It was sweet, gentle, and heartfelt.

I asked him if I could pray one more time as I silently asked the Lord to give me something to encourage him. After I prayed, I told him that I am proud of him, that His heavenly Father is also proud of him, and that he doesn't have to be like his earthly father. I couldn't tell if anything I said hit home for him or not.

We walked back into the tent and his mom asked how it went. I told her what had happened and she was really excited. I asked if he'd like to be baptized and he said he'd like to wait. His mom was thrilled that we had taken the time to minister to him.

Later that night, I was helping with the children's church. This same young man was behaving like a totally different kid. He was running around, hugging kids, playing, smiling, singing the songs, and dancing with us. I believe that his heart was healed because he met with his heavenly Father.

Something that has deeply convicted me is this: how much do I love children? I have heard tons of people say that they don't want to have kids because there are too many people on the earth already or that kids are annoying. I have even said myself that I am not called to children. Yet nowhere in scripture do you find people who ministered only to children, or only to senior citizens, or teenagers. You find people who loved people. They shared the gospel and ministered to everyone regardless of their age, skin tone, or behavior.

Apparently the disciples thought similarly at first, because they tried to keep the kids from disrupting Christ's ministry.

> Then Jesus called for the children and said to the disciples, "Let the children come to me. Don't stop them! For the Kingdom of God belongs to those who are like these children." (Luke 18:16)

> Children are a gift from the Lord;
>   they are a reward from Him. (Psa. 127:3)

Children are a reward? Don't hinder children from coming to Jesus? Here is the deal. Jesus loved children as much as He loved everyone else. They are a part of the same world Jesus came to save that all the rest of us old people are in. We should be thrilled to spend time with kids that aren't our own so that we can show them what it means to follow Jesus like the original disciples did.

Ask yourself these questions. Am I missing out on a blessing because I refuse to have children? Am I missing out on a blessing because I choose not to spend time in kids church, or to hang out with kids and teach them about Jesus? Sure, they are hard work, but when they get it...WOW!

Sometimes I forget that I gave my life to Christ when I was a small boy. I can remember a woman named Sandy Balltosser reading

Pilgrim's Progress and at the end, she asked if anyone wanted to have Jesus live in their heart. I remember praying that prayer for the first time, and truly meaning it. I was eight years old when I got baptized.

Why? Because some crazy old people loved me enough to fight with me every week as I disrupted class, put up with my awful jokes, and faithfully showed me Christ. Today I am a believer, because my parents showed me how to live for Jesus, and a daring woman named Sandy was bold enough to ask a kid if he wanted eternal life.

I have heard people claim that it is not scriptural to say that Jesus comes to "live in your heart" when you're saved. I would like to propose that they may have missed a passage in scripture. Ephesians 3:17 says, "Christ will make his home in your hearts as you trust in Him." "Make His home in your hearts" or "dwell in your hearts" (NASB) is basically the same thing as "live in your heart." Don't make things more complicated than they need to be. We're trying to make the gospel simple for children to understand, and Paul thought it was important enough to say.

Let me tell you, it is not your job to save people. Stop debating whether or not you should talk to kids about Jesus, because they could "walk away from it." That is not your job, that's the Holy Spirit's job. Your job is to point the way and to call out to those kids, "Choose for yourselves today whom you will serve" (Josh. 24:15, NASB).

Maybe some of you are like Sandy, who was incredible with kids. I'd like to say thank you. Thank you for spending countless hours trying to create new ways to keep children's attention. Thank you for the hair you've wanted to rip out of your head as you've been understaffed week after week. Thank you for not quitting on the boys like me who feel compelled to share their silly jokes with their classmates. Keep going.

In the three years I have been with Time to Revive, and the many more that I have been in full time ministry, I know full well that it is crazy difficult to get help with kids during church. We hear it all time, "I don't feel called to kids." They are often considered a distraction instead of a future world changer.

Today ask the Lord to show you a child who needs you to pour into them once in a while. Maybe you could take them for ice cream and ask what Jesus means to them. Maybe you should read *Pilgrim's Progress* to them and ask what they thought. Who knows? The Holy Spirit will show you.

DAY 18
MARSHFIELD, WI

JESUS DOESN'T USE LAYAWAY

A woman came to the evening location and asked for a group of us to pray with her. We all went to this room off to the side so that we wouldn't disturb anyone. When we were done praying with her, a young lady who was with us there wanted us to pray for her as well. She has been a part of the ministry for a while and travels with us all over the place. Her grandmother was there in the room and said we should impart some gifts to her granddaughter.

As we were praying, a team member named Susan had a memory continuously pop into her head. She asked the young lady, "Do you remember a while back when we were out sharing the gospel at a McDonald's, and you told me then that you hadn't really given your life to Christ?"

She said yes, so Susan asked her, "So, have you officially done it yet?"

She answered, "Well...I have prayed the prayer but I haven't really meant it."

It was as if my heart fell right out of my body when she said that. We were all surprised. She had been around so much we just assumed that she was born again already, and yet she hadn't been. We asked her if she was ready, and she said no.

I asked what was keeping her from it and she said, "Because I'm not worthy."

At that moment I felt as if someone stabbed me in the chest. I grabbed the wristband off my wrist, probably more out of habit than anything, and said, "I know you know the gospel. You have traveled the country with your grandma sharing it. So I am not going to go through all of it, but I need you to understand this verse. Romans 5:8 says, 'But God, demonstrates His own love toward us, in that while we were yet sinners, Christ died for us.' What did it cost Jesus to give you eternal life?"

With her head down, she thought about it for a second. Then she looked at me and said, "Everything," choking up a bit on the word.

"When you say you don't think you're 'worthy' of that gift, you need to think about the reality that Jesus considered you worth sacrificing His life in order for you to have eternal life. He gave everything for you to be able to live forever with Him."

Each person in the group shared a word of encouragement they felt the Lord wanted her to know. Finally I asked her again, "After hearing everything that's been spoken here, are you ready to give your life to Jesus?"

"Yes," she said with tears rolling down her cheeks.

I told her that since she shared the gospel all the time, she knew what to do next, so we all closed our eyes, and she prayed the most beautiful prayer, still in tears.

"Wow! Now we can really pray for you!" we said.

1 Timothy 4:14 speaks of imparting spiritual gifts, so we prayed the Lord would give her faith, prophecy, compassion, and discernment. It was incredible. When we were done praying with her, my teammate Garrett felt like he was supposed to give her a hug, to represent her heavenly Father and how happy he was for her.

I asked her if she'd want to get baptized. She immediately said yes! She was smiling ear to ear! We took her outside to the baptism truck, got her a change of clothes, and Garrett baptized her that night!

The rest of the week, she was grinning everywhere she went. She was oozing joy. In fact you could look at her funny, and she would erupt with laughter, because she was filled with the joy of the Lord!

We determine the worth or value of something by what someone is willing to pay for it. I love that our red verse shows us that in the same way you pay for an item before you get it, Jesus paid for us before we became His.

The truth is in some ways, I can understand that because of our sin, and the grime, and the filth we've covered ourselves in, it could heavily affect our value. However even though we were riddled with sin and evil to the core, Jesus loved us enough to die for us. In fact 1 John 3:16 says it like this, "We know what real love is because Jesus gave up His life for us."

Our Father in heaven said, "I think that those people down there are worth my Son as payment." Thousands of people all across America, especially young people, think they aren't worth anything. Why should they? People spend more time telling them all the things they do wrong than what they do well. Let's be determined to encourage others. Let's ask the Lord to help us see people the way He does.

Think about it like this. You just purchased a home. Don't you have the right to paint the walls whatever color you want? Does the home belong to itself? No, that's silly. The home belongs to you.

> Don't you realize that your body is the temple of the Holy Spirit, who lives in you and was given to you by God? You do not belong to yourself, for God bought you with a high price. So you must honor God with your body. (1 Cor. 6:19-20)

Jesus paid for you so that He could live inside of you, which means He now has the right to paint, take out the trash, knock out a few walls, and add a garage. Why? Because He is now the owner of the home. That is what it means for Him to be our Lord. If you are not careful you could look at this as you losing the right to do what you want. And in some ways that's true.

I think a better way to look at it is this. You were the equivalent of a dumpy home that had boarded up windows and looked like it had been burnt to a crisp. Then Jesus showed up and paid the previous owner (who wasn't you by the way, He just let you pretend like you were) way more than it was technically worth. The old owner moved out and the new one moved in. He put up new siding and new windows. He's redoing the roof, and renovating the kitchen.

Months later the old owner shows up, very confused. The place resembles nothing of what it used to. Why? Because when Jesus looks at our mess He says, "I can work with that. I want him." There is no fixer-upper that He is too scared to take on.

> God paid a high price for you, so don't be enslaved by the world. (1 Cor. 7:23)

Now, I realize that both of these scriptures from Corinthians are in the context of controlling your body instead of indulging in sexual immorality. Most of chapter 7 is discussing whether or not you should get married, but in three verses, including verse 23, Paul is talking about human masters and slaves. There he makes it clear that if you have the opportunity to be free from the world, you should take it. You have been purchased with the blood of Jesus.

What I want you to realize is this. Jesus considers us valuable enough to pay that high price. He didn't say, "Look, I will purchase everyone else but you." No! He paid for the world's salvation with one swoop.

Today while you're out and about, look for someone downtrodden. Speak life into them and tell them their value, according to the checkbook of heaven and not your own opinions.

RESPONSE

DAY 19
JASPER, IN

CLUTZ FOR JESUS

Sometimes before we go out to evangelize, I will make a list of all the impressions the Lord gave us while we were praying. This particular day I was with a group of people that had never been out before. We sat in my car to pray and then I asked if the Lord had put anything on anyone's heart. They gave me their responses and I wrote them down in my notes app on my phone. One of the people on my team mentioned a Hucks gas station and Walmart.

We were headed in the direction of the closest Walmart when we saw a Hucks. We pulled in, excited to see what we would find. We walked around the store and bought a drink as we asked the Lord to show us someone to encounter.

There was one person in particular that stood out to two of us guys, but it was a girl and we thought we should have the lady with us to talk to her, but she was outside. We went to the lady on our team and told her about the girl we thought we were supposed to encounter, but as we turned around, the girl was getting into her car and driving away. We thought we had botched the whole thing. We discussed as a team whether or not us guys should have just talked to her ourselves.

We were pretty discouraged, but we weren't going to quit. There were still people at the gas station, but none of us felt the need to stay. So we got into the car and headed to Walmart.

We were in the middle of nowhere, where it takes a while to get from one place to another. We were using the time in the car to get to know each other and enjoying what the Lord had been doing in each of our lives, when all of a sudden one of the guys in the back seat yells, "There's another Hucks!"

It scared me so badly, I whipped the car to the left and flew into the gas station. There was only one other car there, so I pulled up to the same pump they were at, but on the opposite side. I saw that there were two guys standing by the car, so I told my team, "I will put gas in my car so that we have the 'right' to be here, and you go talk to the guys."

We all got out of the car and as I paid for gas at the pump, I could hear one of the guys hanging up the nozzle (if that's the right term) and getting into the car. I told the team, "Now is your chance, go talk to them!"

They just stood there frozen, with blank looks on their faces. I was trying to put the nozzle into my car and I heard the second car door slam closed. Everything inside me screamed, "If you don't go now, we will miss them too!"

So I leapt over the hose (this is necessary for those of us with short legs), but one of my feet got caught. I basically fell around the corner of the pump and as I was falling I saw that their rear passenger window was open. I slammed my hand on the trunk of their car, both to keep from falling on my face and to grab their attention, and yelled as best as I could, "HEY!"

The guy sitting in the passenger seat opened the door to look at me as I was trying to get up, my foot still tangled in the hose. "How can I help you?" he asked, and I am sure that I looked like a fool.

I tried to stand as I said, "This is going to sound ridiculous, so I am warning you in advance. We were praying for the Lord to show us who we could pray for and He told us to go to a Hucks. We were laughing and carrying on in the car when all of a sudden one of the guys in the back seat screamed at me that there was a Hucks and I just found myself whipping the car into the parking lot. Man, you guys are the only ones here, and I believe that we were sent here to talk to you."

At this point my foot was free and I made my way to the passenger's side door, which was still open, to address both guys. "I know we are extra strange and I didn't set out to yell at you or slam my hand on your car...but is there anything going on in your lives that you could use prayer for?"

They just laughed and said we really weren't as strange as we thought. Then they began to explain that they did need prayer, and that it was a "coincidence" that we would show up. The driver asked if we could pray for him because a gas leak was found in his house and he didn't have any family or anywhere to go in the area, and he was worried that they would condemn his house. He didn't want to be homeless. The passenger said he wanted prayer for his kids. They lived with their mom and she was neglecting them because she spent more time sleeping around and doing drugs than taking care of them.

Immediately my heart went out to these guys. My team came closer and we prayed for them, kneeling on the ground in between the car and the gas pump. After we prayed, we asked if we could give them a gift to remind them that we prayed, and they looked surprised. I told them that if it was too wierd or lame, they didn't have to accept it until after they saw it. They agreed so we got wristbands from the car, because we had forgotten to grab them with everything happening so fast.

They said the wristbands were cool and seemed grateful, so we asked if they had a minute or two so we could explain the colors. They looked at the clock in their car and said they had some time, as they looked at each other, smiling. We handed them Bibles, and I switched knees, because the pavement indention was starting to hurt.

We walked them through each color, and as we got to blue the driver said he didn't believe God existed. He was officially an atheist, and he went on and on about how much research he had done and when he was in jail he read all these books, and that if he had to choose a religion at all it would be Buddhism over Christianity any day.

When I asked why that was, he explained, "Christians don't even do what Jesus taught, so why in the world would I want to join a religion that consists primarily of people who also don't believe it enough to do what their leader said. You guys are the only people I have ever met who say they're Christians and are actually trying to live like Jesus said. I don't agree with you at all, but I do believe you believe this stuff," he said, waving the Bible and looking me in the eyes.

I thanked him and we continued to the last verse. They had both made it very clear they did not want to get saved, so when we were finished with the green verse, I thanked them for their time and went to stand to leave. (Because I had been kneeling since I had prayed for him, I got up like an old man.) Everything I knew to do was now done, and in my brain, we were finished.

As I was standing up, one of them said, "Hey, there is one more color!"

"Yeah," I said, "but that is for people who want to follow Jesus, and you guys made it pretty clear you don't want to do that."

"Can we see it anyways?"

I couldn't see a reason not to let them know what it said. It's not a top secret tab that you have to have clearance in order to read, so I bent back down and started walking them through it. I explained that when you get saved, you're sealed with the Holy Spirit and you become a new creation. I told them that when people do that, the Holy Spirit starts to clean up their lives instead of them trying to do it all on their own.

We told them about baptism and how it's a symbol declaring your faith to your community and to the world. Then we explained discipleship and how that could include going to church, but is more referring to finding someone to meet with regularly who can show you how to be like Jesus.

"We want that," the driver said.

"Huh?" I literally said, shocked out of my mind.

"We want that," he said again as the passenger nodded his head in agreement.

"Uhhh... You want someone to meet with you to talk to you about how to be like Jesus?" I asked, still confused.

"Yeah, we want that," they said.

"You know that whoever meets with you is going to ask you again if you want to get saved right?"

"Yeah, we know"

"Uhhh, ok... Well, let me get your contact information."

I reached into my pocket and opened up my phone. They asked if they could keep the Bibles, because they were really cool.

"Of course," I said, trying to understand what in the world was happening.

They gave us their contact information and thanked us for stopping and talking to them. They said they needed to get going and we told them that we would continue to pray for their situations, and that I believed good things were down the road.

There is a really important story for us to check out in Acts 17. There we see Paul in the city of Athens where he spent time sharing the gospel with their philosophers, but they didn't really understand what he was trying to say. Those philosophers took him to what is called the "high council" (v. 19). As he addresses the council, he is looking around and notices they have all sorts of statues and shrines, as well as a place for a god they don't even know. He gives a brief account of Israel's history and then explains the gospel. At the end of the speech this is what happens.

> When they heard Paul speak about the resurrection of the dead, some laughed in contempt, but others said, "We want to hear more about this later." That ended Paul's discussion with them, but some joined him and became believers. (vv. 32-34)

People are going to have various responses to the gospel. In this story in Acts, there are three responses from those who heard Paul's presentation. Some thought it was a joke, some wanted to hear more, and some believed. This second response was like the guys in my story. Even though they didn't decide to get saved that day, they were still interested in hearing more.

Sometimes that is what it takes. You never know what will happen to someone when they go home and think things over. You don't know if God will show up to them in a dream or send another person to them five minutes after they leave you. Do not allow the decision to wait to discourage you, in fact it should thrill you. It means they are carefully weighing what they are about to do. In my experience, those who wait and don't rush into it are the most likely to really dive in and follow Christ wholeheartedly.

Something else I'd like to point out (since I have you here), is that those who scoffed did so "when they heard Paul speak about the resurrection of the dead." Why would they scoff at that? Well, because it's pretty much insane. To the Athenians, and really to most of us here in America, people rising from the dead after having been buried for three days doesn't happen every Monday, which is why it is so incredibly hard to believe. It's the same reaction some young people get when they tell their parents they believe mermaids exist. To the hearer, it sounds like you belong in a nuthouse. For the Christian, the matter of the resurrection is essential, and salvation cannot occur without believing that Jesus was in fact, raised from the dead.

We need to be aware that some people won't only reject the message, but they will be blatantly disrespectful. When that happens, we do need to love those people, but focus instead on the ones that are interested. Paul could've spent whole days, for weeks on end, trying to figure out how to convince the mockers, but that's not what he did. Paul took the guys who wanted to know more and he poured himself into them, showing them the way.

Can you imagine how Paul might have felt being laughed at? It probably didn't feel good, but the truth of the matter is that we don't see his feelings being mentioned, only that he stayed the course and didn't back down when he was in a position where he easily could have compromised.

Today as you pray, ask the Lord if you're in a place where you would be willing to look foolish for the gospel. Do you need to have everything all together or can God use you the way you are? Ask the Lord to show you or remind you of people who might be in that stage where they haven't believed yet, but they're interested. You could have a good conversation with them where you represent the gospel or just check in with them.

Maybe you're in a position where you have been laughed at when you shared your faith, and you've allowed it to shut you down. Maybe you prayed for someone in public and it went terribly and you're afraid to try again because someone could laugh at you. If that is you, you are in good company. Thank you for trying. It is time to try again.

Don't allow fear of what others might say and do stop you from declaring an eternity changing message. For one soul, I will be laughed at. For one soul, I will be mocked. My eyes have been opened to what happens in eternity. We need to forgive those who have hurt our feelings when we put ourselves out there, and we need to repent for allowing that to shut us down.

Today let's take a step of bold faith, and find someone to share this amazing message with! Like Paul said, Jesus is alive!

DAY 20
HAMMOND, IN

JESUS TAKE THE WHEEL

You may remember my friend Garrett from some earlier stories that took place at reviveWisconsin. Garrett's car was having some issues, so he borrowed a vehicle for us to use on the trip. On the way home from Wisconsin, I was driving through Hammond, Indiana on highway 80/94. We'd just pulled onto the Indianapolis Boulevard exit ramp when the car started acting strangely. The wheel was super hard to turn.

"Garrett!" I said, "The power steering went out!"

I made it off the highway and saw a Walmart right there so we pulled in, and of course, Walmart was out of what we needed. They told us to go to this AutoZone down the road right past the construction. Before we left the Walmart parking lot, Garrett and I checked how much fluid was in the reservoir, and it was completely dry. We checked it two times.

So at the advice of the man who didn't have what we needed, we went off on an adventure to try to find AutoZone. We reached out to a few people about what had happened, and had our wives and some other friends praying for us while we tried to safely find an AutoZone.

We drove all the way down to the other end of town and into Whiting, the next town over, where there are no AutoZones. Finally, we just looked for one on the GPS and started to head toward it. The problem was that it required us to turn a lot more, which was of course difficult without power steering. We were praying as we drove and trying to joke about the whole situation, when all of a sudden, the wheel started to turn with ease again.

I told Garrett, since I was still driving, "Garrett! The wheel is turning! It's working!"

We got to AutoZone, checked the dipstick, and what do you know? It was dripping with fluid! We bought some more to fill it up the rest of the way. I believe the Lord put fluid back into our steering system specifically so that we could make it to AutoZone.

P.S. Garrett has been around cars his whole life and is confident we checked the right reservoir. I asked a mechanic friend (he's not a Christian, so I know he's unbiased) if there is any explanation for this to have happened. His response was "fluid can't just appear." As I went into more detail about what happened and how, he just looked at me in disbelief.

One day, when there was a large crowd following Jesus, He told his disciples to do something crazy. With hardly enough to feed themselves, let alone thousands of people, Jesus told the disciples to feed the crowd. They had everyone sit in an orderly fashion, and after Jesus blessed the food we read this.

> Then, breaking the loaves into pieces, He gave the bread to the disciples, who distributed it to the people. They all ate as much as they wanted, and afterward, the disciples picked up twelve baskets of leftovers. (Matt. 14:19-20)

Here in Matthew we see that Jesus provided for the need by telling the disciples to act as though they had the provision already.

That is why he had them organize the crowd in a way that would allow them to distribute the food quickly and efficiently. Then Jesus was able to take what they had and multiply it.

In our story we have a modern example of God's provision. Garrett and I reached out to some people who agreed with us in prayer and God showed up by putting fluid in our car. I believe that He honors our faith in Him when we ask for something that may seem silly to a lot of people. We didn't create fluid out of anywhere. We aren't that skilled. But Jesus is. God spoke the universe into existence. Why would it be so hard to believe that He can create steering fluid? Because they were following Jesus, the disciples were able to be a part of God's miraculous provision.

It is my belief that if we are also doing the will of our heavenly Father, we too will be able to be a part of the miracles He wants to do. For about eight months before this story happened, I had been praying about the gift of miracles. I am not saying that I believe that that the fluid reappeared because of these prayers, but I am saying that it was a confirmation for me to keep praying. Keep seeking the Lord so that you can testify about the goodness and greatness of Jesus showing up in your life too.

Another thing to consider is this. In John 14 Jesus is dealing with people on whether or not they really believe He was sent by the Father. But He goes on to say,

> "I tell you the truth, anyone who believes in me will do the same works I have done, and even greater works, because I am going to be with the Father. You can ask for anything in my name, and I will do it, so that the Son can bring glory to the Father." (John 14:12-13)

It would be silly to think that Jesus was not referring to the supernatural when He said this, especially after just saying that they should believe the Father sent Him because of the "works" He was doing. By no means do I think that having steering fluid appear in the car was a greater work than the ones Jesus did, but I think it's a step in that direction.

Jesus says we can ask for "anything" in His name and it will be done. It is my conviction that If we are in a situation where God would be glorified by a "work" being done, I believe He will answer that.

The point of miracles, and signs, and wonders, and the gifts of the Spirit is to see people saved and the church edified, and according to verse 13, "so that the Son can bring glory to the Father," not so that you can become the next latest and greatest sideshow.

Today ask yourself this question, do I believe miracles still happen today? Why or why not? Am I remotely interested in seeing the miraculous? Position your heart today to be open to miracles in your life. Humble yourself. If you're not seeing these signs and wonders, ask yourself if you're even hungry to see. If you are hungry, keep putting yourself in a position for God to show up, and He will, especially when it's for His Kingdom and His glory.

DAY 21
ELKHART, IN

THE LIBRARY GOSPEL

When I was learning to share the gospel using the Time to Revive method, I would always try to get on teams with older ladies. Growing up I had been taught that a move of God happens because of the lady prayer warriors. There is this amazing woman who was (and still is) traveling with Revive named Valita. At the time of this story, Valita was living in Ohio and had traveled to my city to share the gospel.

"Wow," I thought, "She isn't on staff, and she still travels to each city as a volunteer?"

Valita had this notebook with all the names of everyone she was ever on a team with, and all the people she prayed or shared the gospel with. Man! Valita is the real deal. She loves the Lord, loves people, and is humble.

On to the story.

My team ended up at the library in downtown Elkhart. Now, I am the last guy on earth who belongs in a library (not because I don't like to read, but because libraries are traditionally quiet, and my thoughts are louder than most people's whispers). (It would also be true that I don't really enjoy reading, which makes it funny that I wrote a book.) There was an area where a group of teenagers were sitting and eating Wendy's, so I decided to go over and see what would happen.

When I first started sharing the gospel, I would psych myself up before I approached someone. I would tell myself that I'm a pretty neat guy, I'm sort of funny, and surely these people will love what I have to say. Arrogant or not, I really did that. I have realized since then that I'm actually not very interesting at all, not funny, and the valuable things I have to say are things I have plagiarized from the Bible!

I sat down to interact with these three teens and nobody was paying attention to me. All my jokes fell flat. There was only one girl showing an interest, and would respond to me here and there. As I started to talk to the girl to find out how I could pray for her, I asked what her name was, and she clearly told me a guy's name. I was shocked. My face probably demonstrated what was going through my mind.

It was a guy, who dressed and looked like a girl…long hair up in a ponytail and makeup on his face, and who asked me to refer to him using male pronouns instead of female. I kept apologizing to for using the wrong pronouns, because to be honest, I have never in my life interacted with someone like this before. I said, "In my defense, you do look like a girl" and he responded that that was fair.

After a while, Valita came over at the same time that he agreed to go through the wristband. We walked through the gospel with him and after he had read all the verses, he told us that he didn't believe that anyone loved him. He began to tell us about his childhood to prove it. He told us about how his parents gave him up to the foster care system because they didn't want him. He had other siblings that they didn't get rid of, only him. In the last year or so, his parents felt guilty for doing it, so they brought him out of the system. Even while he had been in foster care, he would go from house to house because the families didn't want him.

"Churches don't even want me," he said. "Every church I go to…they kick me out right away. I believe there is a God, but I don't believe anyone loves me."

That's when Valita kicked into high gear. She raised her voice at him, "What did it say?! Read it again!" She had him go back through the verses. "We all sin. So what if you struggle with homosexuality, we all have vices."

She pointed her finger in my shoulder and said, "Jesse sins, I sin, we all sin! It doesn't matter what kind of sin it is, we all sin, and we have all earned death! None of us escape that! But because God loved us, He sent His Son to die in our place while we were living in sin!"

As I listened to her words, the Holy Spirit grabbed my heart. Tears started to come to my eyes as I realized that my sin was self-righteousness. She was right. Without Christ's gift of eternal life, I would be screwed! I would be hopeless!

She went on to say, "Don't tell me God doesn't love you, when it says right here that He does!"

This young man rejected the gospel. To be absolutely honest, I realized that I didn't really love this guy. I knew that I should, but I didn't. My mindset up to that point was that this kid was reaping what he was sowing, but I didn't really care who he was. I didn't care that he was a lost, hurting, misdirected young man, crying out for someone to love him.

That day changed my life. I have never looked at people the same. When I see them my heart is filled with compassion, regardless of their circumstances or the kinds of sin they deal with. It still breaks my heart to this day to think about this young man's decision. Even now, my heart burns for another chance to talk to him, to share the love with him that I should have had the first time, regardless of the lifestyle choices he makes.

The church is incredibly divided over the theology of homosexuality. My understanding of scripture is that we all sin. Regardless if your vice is sexuality, drunkenness, or lying, it's appalling in the sight of God. He doesn't look down and say cheating on your wife is more awful than being gay. Jesus said this when talking about what defiles a person's heart, "For from the heart come evil thoughts, murder, adultery, all sexual immorality, theft, lying, and slander" (Matt. 15:19).

The truth about homosexuality is this: God loves the people who are trapped in that lifestyle, and through the power that raised Jesus from the dead, anyone who deals with ANY kind of sexual sin has access to the power that can help them not to sin. You have to make a choice regardless of your sexual orientation, to do what's right. We all have sexual tendencies built into us and God gives us the ability, through the fruit of the Spirit, to be able to control those desires.

However, I do not hold people who do not profess Christ as their Lord to live to the same standards as Christians. Because of this encounter, I now have a love for people who live this alternate lifestyle that allows me to talk to them, and it doesn't faze me. They're just lost people doing what lost people do, and they need Jesus.

Jesus spent his time with the outcasts of society, and called them to righteousness through repentance. My hope is to do the same. To love people enough not to leave them in their sin, but to call them unto righteousness. I love the story of the woman caught in adultery in John 8, because it shows me Christ's response to any kind of sin. You're not condemned by him. Verse 11 says, "Go and sin no more." Jesus would not have commanded the lady to sin no more if she was incapable of doing so.

Today as you read this story, I wonder who around you is bound by sexual sin? Sometimes it's hidden, but a lot of times it's been broadcasted. Maybe you're sitting here and you're dealing with hidden sexual sin. Maybe you have been consumed with pornography and you have grown to hate yourself but you find yourself bound. Maybe you think you're getting away with it, because "it isn't hurting anyone."

You think nobody knows, but what you don't realize is that it has infiltrated the way you treat the opposite sex. You have become a selfish prick, taking what you want without any restraint. REPENT.

Whether you have found yourself bound and you're living it up or you want out of it, either way, God sees every single immoral thought you have. He knows that you are cheating on your spouse in your mind. Stop it! Repent. Get help, if you need it. There are churches and ministries that help people develop the self-discipline necessary to say no when those instances present themselves.

I love how Proverbs 5 and 7 say it. These two chapters are written from a father to his son and he basically says, "See that girl over there? Stay away! She's a trap! You touch her and you're gonna die! Get a wife and rejoice in her. Keep yourself for her and don't spread yourself around!"

Practically speaking, If you're reading this and you find yourself struggling with any form of sexual sin, whether you are homosexual or heterosexual, addicted to porn or not, I believe that God can set you free from that. Repent. Ask the Holy Spirit to give you self control, and then practice saying no. After you repent, tell someone. Find another person who will hold you accountable. Do not tell someone who isn't going to call you and ask if you messed up.

One of the greatest things you can do is memorize scripture and preach to yourself. Psalm 119:11 says, "I have hidden your word in my heart, that I might not sin against you." I believe this works with any sin that you may struggle with, whether it's sexual in nature or not. As you hide the Word in your heart, you will find you don't have time to think the way you used to think. You will find that your heart is being transformed and your speech is going to change because what used to fill your heart was vile, and now it's filled with righteousness.

You need to be delivered. Sometimes you need a drill sergeant and other times you need someone to hold your hand. I believe that some of you will be delivered in an instant. But most of you will have to fight for your deliverance. There is so much grace for you if you want out of that. Some of you are going to have to break up with your partner. Some of you will have to get married so that you're not living in sin. All of us who are saved have the power that raised Christ from the dead living inside us, so we have the power to break the chains of sin in us. We have to submit to that.

As you go out today, be aware there could be sexual sin in the person you encounter. Don't run away scared if they are living a sexually immoral lifestyle. Pray for them, and then go talk to them. Offer them the opportunity to be set free. Call them to follow Jesus and to live righteously by being born again.

DAY 22
DARKE COUNTY, OH

LIGHT IN THE DARKE

When we were in Darke County, this amazing man donated a semi-truck load of watermelons for us to give away while we shared the gospel. Every once in a while our team will send teams out in the evening so that people who work during the day can have the opportunity to learn how to share the gospel. This particular evening, my job was to hand out watermelons to the teams as they came out of the building. People would pull up their vehicles and I would shove as many melons as I could into their trunks.

After all the teams had left, a few of us decided to go out and see what the Lord would do. My wife Elly, a guy named Greg, and I took some melons to try to give them away. Sometimes the Lord leads us to a specific place, and other times we just drive to see where we'd end up.

This time we ended up at an apartment building. We tried to give the melons away, but nobody really wanted them, or our prayers. So we went door to door across the street from the apartments.

We knocked on a door, and then argued about which one of us should stand in front of the door. It's awkward for everyone involved, so we had my wife do it, since she's more visually appealing than us men. A man came to the door as he was heading out to smoke. We asked him if he would like a watermelon. At first he was hesitant, because he assumed there was a catch.

"Not with us," we told him, "We just need to get rid of them, and if you'd like, we could pray for you while we're here."

When he realized they were free, he said he would take as many as we had with us. So we unloaded the vehicle at his house, and hung out with him as he smoked. At some point while we were bringing the watermelons, the man's wife came to the door too.

We were able to pray with them, and found out that they were already Christians. Their prayer request was for their teenage daughter who had attempted suicide only a few days earlier. After we prayed for them, we asked if their daughter was home and if she would be interested in meeting with us.

They invited us in and called their daughter. We greeted her and explained who we were, why we were there, and that we just wanted to pray with her. She and my wife were really able to connect. She shared what she had been going through that led her to making the decision to try to end her life, but that she regretted it as soon as she had done it. Our team poured into her and prayed with her. We gave her a Bible and band and walked her through the gospel.

One of the things that I felt the Lord pressing me to share was the fruit of the Spirit. I opened our little blue Bible to that passage in Galatians 5 and had her read it. I explained that when she gives her life to the Lord, the Holy Spirit will fill her and the natural outcome is love, joy, peace, patience, kindness, goodness, faithfulness, gentleness, and self control (v. 22).

We explained that what she really needed was the peace and joy that comes from Jesus. We often seek these things out in the wrong places, but Jesus is the only one who can really give you peace that passes understanding. This young lady decided to follow Jesus, and my wife had the privilege to lead her in the sinner's prayer.

Recently I saw an advertisement for a book on how to get the gospel back into youth ministry. My first thought was, "Father forgive us for removing the gospel from our youth." We have focused on games, entertainment, and snacks more than we have on giving them life eternal.

It seems that the only version of evangelism most of the American church is familiar with involves showing Christian movies that end up only being attended by people in their own congregations. Some churches really do try to reach out through social justice programs like soup kitchens or offering temporary housing for those in need. Please, don't get rid of that soup kitchen, but for heaven's sake, share the gospel.

Young people everywhere are killing themselves because they see no light at the end of the tunnel. But there is hope to be had. There is a fruit that leads to eternal life.

In 2015 my wife had a dream. It was about all these hungry people coming to the church, and they would find these beautiful fruits, but as they took bites out of them they found that the fruit was filled with insects.

I believe that dream was a picture of the church in America. We have spent more time figuring out how to have the latest and greatest light show and the best coffee, than we have in preaching the Word of God and calling people into righteous living. We have been offering fruit that looks good, but is rotten and decaying inside. The world needs hope, and that's why suicide rates are so high. If the church isn't offering it, where will they get it? Outside of Jesus there is no hope.

I want to make sure that you understand a few things. I am not a doctor. In fact, I am far from it. There is nothing wrong with seeking help from a licensed doctor or counselor for help with depression or suicidal tendencies, yet there is a lot of confusion out there on the topic of suicide. Most of the church spends more time arguing about whether or not the person who commits suicide goes to heaven than trying to bring hope to those who want to end it all.

There are a lot of reasons people struggle and it is my belief that what these people need so desperately is not our opinions, or telling them to "deal with it" or to "get over it," but a reason to hope. "Why should I not kill myself?" They are begging for us to answer. It is my absolute position that they need an encounter with Jesus.

> The LORD is close to the brokenhearted;
> He rescues those whose spirits are crushed. (Psa. 34:18)

I think that if we pay attention to this passage we can learn a lot about how to help those who deal with depression and suicide.

"The Lord is close." Man, I cannot tell you how many times I have sat with a depressed person who tells me that they feel alone. They withdraw from everyone, not necessarily because they want to throw a pity party for themselves, but because there is a war going on in their minds. They withdraw because they think there is something wrong with them and that nobody loves them.

Jesus is close to those who are brokenhearted. Whether it's because her jerkwad boyfriend broke up with her, or a spouse was cheating, or he just found out he has cancer, a broken heart is a broken heart. We need to carry their burdens with them, not stare and gawk and gossip about them. Come close to them and let them know the Lord is right there with them. They aren't alone.

Next, we see that "He rescues those whose spirits are crushed." This is not something I believe we can do. We can run into burning buildings and carry people out. We can dive into oceans where people are drowning and pull them out. But I believe only the Lord can rescue a crushed spirit. The way we can facilitate this is to sit with those struggling, hold their hands, and pray with them.

Ask Jesus to reveal himself, ask Him to tell them what HE says about them. Have them ask Jesus if there are any lies they've been believing and what truth they need to believe instead.

> Give all your worries and cares to God, for He cares about you. (1 Pet. 5:7)

In my experience, depression and suicide become the proverbial fruits that grow on the worry/anxiety tree. Many of those dealing with depression have gotten into a habit of worrying and not releasing it to the Lord, so it builds and builds, and then it starts messing with their minds.

Maybe they don't give their worries to the Lord because of fundamental trust issues, fear, and control. If the Lord is in control, than I am not. It may not become depression right away, but the fruit of holding onto control instead of giving it to the Lord will probably end up there eventually.

We need to gently lead them in handing those worries and cares to God. Many times they get so caught up in the pain of their brokenness that they can't think clearly enough to even make that decision on their own. You can help them through that. It could look something like this, "Jesus, I give my worry/concern/anxiety about _____ to You."

Philippians 4 has been the most helpful passage in dealing with the hard times in my own life, and I have seen an incredible effect on people dealing with suicidal thoughts as these scriptures fill them with hope. There is a lot in this chapter, but I want to break some of it down for you.

> Always be full of joy in the Lord. I say it again—rejoice! (v.4)

When life is in chaos, and we just want to binge on Netflix and comfort foods, or when it's even worse and we hide in our rooms under the covers hoping nobody will bother us, even as we get lost in the lies of our minds, we are told to rejoice. Not because we're thrilled that life sucks, but because even in the midst of brokenness and worry, "remember, the Lord is coming soon" (v.5) and He is still good. It may not seem like it, but He is.

In verses 6-9, Paul gives a practical list of steps to take to arrive at peace, which leads to joy.

> Then you will experience God's peace, which exceeds anything we can understand. His peace will guard your hearts and minds as you live in Christ Jesus. (v.7)

You may be reading this and you too are dealing with depression or suicidal thoughts. The steps and simple prayers listed will work for you too. Don't be afraid or ashamed to talk to someone and have them pray with you about it.

Lamentations says it really well. Jeremiah wrote this book while he was agonizing over the condition of his people who were being enslaved by Babylon.

> I will never forget this awful time
>   as I grieve over my loss.
> Yet I still dare to hope
>   when I remember this:

The faithful love of the Lord never ends!
    His mercies never cease.
Great is His faithfulness;
    His mercies begin afresh each morning.
I say to myself, "The Lord is my inheritance;
    therefore I will hope in Him!" (Lam. 3:20-24)

We have misplaced our hope. We have put it in individuals who will endlessly fail us. The Lord's love is faithful. It doesn't end when you fall, and it never runs out. His faithfulness is great. The reason you can live for tomorrow is because your hope is in your inheritance, which is the Lord. I love that. It means that until He takes me home, I have something to do here.

Today as we pray before we leave our homes, let's ask the Lord to open our eyes to those around us dealing with suicidal thoughts. Ask the Lord to give you insights to who they are and how you can encourage them. John 10:10 tells us that the devil is a liar and he comes to "steal, kill, and destroy." He'd like nothing better than have you dead, but Jesus has a plan for you and He wants to give you "a rich and satisfying life."

RESPONSE

DAY 23
GOSHEN, IN

WE MAY HAVE STOLEN SOMETHING

My friend here in the Goshen area has been leading a regular Wednesday evening outreach at his church, so I decided to join him and encourage their crew. The week before at a local coffee shop, I had met some people from his church who were really excited about hitting the streets. They have a small crew, but they are faithful.

The team I ended up on was sort of moseying through town, because we hadn't really had any ideas of where to go. There is a laundromat downtown, so as we drove past, our driver decided to give it a shot. We parked the car, and two of us went inside while the other two stayed to pray. I was on the prayer team.

While my teammate and I were praying, I noticed a man and a woman looking at some cabinets on the side of the street. I couldn't tell if they were for sale or what from the car, but I felt led to go check out the situation.

We walked across the street and I called out to the people, "Hey, do you know if these cabinets are for sale?"

They said they didn't know and that's what they were trying to find out. The woman had been knocking on the door of the house, but nobody answered.

In our area if someone wants to get rid of something they put it by the street, usually marked with a sign telling people to take whatever it is. There was no sign, as far as we could tell, and since it was the city, there's a good chance the people put the cabinets there for the city to pick up. So we determined that they were most likely free or trash. The couple really wanted them because they were nicer than the ones they had. I told them that we might be able to help. I saw that my teammates had come out of the laundromat so I called over to them to help.

Our driver had a truck, so we loaded up the cabinets in the bed, but before we took them to his house (which was literally on the next block), we asked them how we could pray. They were shocked that we would do that, and said nobody had asked them that before. Then we drove over to their house and helped them unload everything. They were so thankful for our help and repeatedly told us so. They were thrilled to have new cabinets.

We asked if we could give them a gift to remind them that we prayed for them and helped with the cabinets. They gladly accepted the wristband. We asked if we could explain the colors and they were thrilled, but because it was super dark out, we couldn't see very well. At first, we tried to use the lights on our phones, but it really wasn't working well. The husband spoke Spanish as his first language, and he was struggling with seeing and reading, so they invited us into their home so we could see better.

This couple had three kids and they lived in a tiny apartment, but they were excited to have us. We filled their dining room, and went through the Bible and band with the whole family.

When we were on the blue verse the mom told us that she had been to church a lot growing up, but she got tired of people judging her so she left. Her husband was from Mexico (woohoo!) and he had never been to church. They told us that they didn't mind if their kids went, and that they attended a Wednesday evening kids program at the church across the street. All the kids loved to go.

As we explained the gospel, you could see that they were really getting it. When we finished, we asked them if they wanted the gift of eternal life and they all said yes! Our team led the entire family through a prayer and took the time to discuss what it means to be born again (the orange tab), and how now they have the Holy Spirit inside them. We asked them if they would like to meet regularly with one of the people on our team to talk about life and the Bible, and they excitedly agreed.

Sometimes you have to meet a tangible need in order to share the gospel (this isn't foolproof, but for the most part it really works). In our American culture, people are hesitant to talk to unfamiliar people. "Stranger danger" is taught in our schools, and here we are telling you to go be a non-dangerous stranger, to go love on people you don't know. It is absolutely counter-culture. We recognize that the only people who do anything sort of like this are the Mormons and Jehovah's Witnesses, and IT IS WEIRD, which is okay. Weird doesn't mean wrong.

Because nobody really does this, we have to help break down the awkwardness. Helping someone move cabinets is a great way to do that. You could mow the grass, pull weeds, or whatever else will help someone to overcome the awkwardness. Personally, I try to tell a lot of jokes and get them laughing, which usually works (not always, you do have to use discernment).

> If someone has enough money to live well and sees a brother
> or sister in need but shows no compassion—how can God's
> love be in that person? (1 John 3:17)

Jesus tells a parable in Luke 10 similar to the one I just told about a Good Samaritan. Sure, we didn't have to clean up a half-dead naked guy and put him up in a hotel, but the principle is the same. There were three guys in His story. Two of them held positions of religious stature, but neither of them stopped to help.

> "Then a despised Samaritan came along, and when he saw
> the man, he felt compassion for him. Going over to him, the
> Samaritan soothed his wounds with olive oil and wine and
> bandaged them. Then he put the man on his own donkey and

took him to an inn, where he took care of him. The next day he handed the innkeeper two silver coins, telling him, 'Take care of this man. If his bill runs higher than this, I'll pay you the next time I'm here.'

"Now which of these three would you say was a neighbor to the man who was attacked by bandits?" Jesus asked.

The man replied, "The one who showed him mercy."

Then Jesus said, "Yes now go and do the same." (Luke 10:33-37)

The concept of this story is that a guy who, according to culture, wasn't supposed to associate with the half-dead naked guy on the side of the road was the one that helped, and the so-called righteous guys passed by, even though they had the means to do something. Jesus' point is that we need to show mercy to people in a position of need.

There we were, helping people who didn't have a car get some cabinets down the street so that they didn't have to make a hundred trips, it was a small thing for us to do, but it opened the door.

Today as you're driving around town, keep your eyes open. You can't see the needs around you if your eyes aren't open to what is going on. That sounds ridiculously obvious, but the reality is, we pass people all the time who are desperate and we "see" what's happening, but because we don't see through eyes of mercy, we pass them without a thought.

There's a car on the side of the road. They need help changing a tire. You can help. Even if you don't know how to, that doesn't mean you can't pull over and ask if there is anything you can do. Maybe they need a ride. Maybe their phone isn't working and they need help calling someone. You'll never know until you stop.

Now, please, please, please be aware that there are people out there that intentionally take advantage of Good Samaritans. This is why it's important to pray and discern while you're looking for someone to help. There are people who are evil and have used the roadside car problem to bait people. I have also heard that in larger cities, it's common for criminals to put babies in strollers and leave them all alone, then as people (usually women) check on the baby and look for the mother, they are kidnapped, or raped, or murdered.

In the story of the Good Samaritan I'd like to point out that there is one innocent guy who gets robbed/beaten/stripped/left for dead, two guys who do not stop to help, one guy who does stop to help, and then an unnumbered amount of "bandits." There could have been two bandits or ten, but either way, this story would not have happened without them. If there were not evil people out there setting out to destroy lives, there wouldn't be as many opportunities for Good Samaritans.

So yes, be warned that there are people who hurt people. We need to pray for their salvation and imprisonment. But we can not allow ourselves to be fearful of them or stop helping others because of the potential that we could be harmed.

Now, I think this is part of why Jesus sent out His disciples in twos, so that together you can discern, along with the Holy Spirit, whether or not you should stop. It would be very hard for me to ignore a baby alone on the street. Maybe the response should be to watch from a distance and call the police? Maybe it is to check on it and find the mother? I don't know all the answers but the Holy Spirit who guides us does. Trust Him.

Don't be afraid to help those in need. In Jesus' words, "go and do the same" as the Samaritan guy. Go show mercy today. Wash some dishes, change a tire, buy some ice cream, open a door. Who knows where it will lead.

DAY 24
ABILENE, TX

LOOK UP

In many cities we are invited into businesses, sports teams and schools to share the gospel. This particular day we were invited to a local college's Fellowship of Christian Athletes, or FCA, meeting. Sometimes we do a presentation to the entire group and sometimes we break it up and do one-on-one, depending on what best fits the situation. Because this particular FCA ends their sessions in smaller groups, we were able to share with each group as they dismissed. The students are given the option to stay or go after their group is finished.

My teammate caught a group of girls as they were leaving and asked if they'd like a Bible and band before they left. They did, so I went with her to talk to them. We gave them the wristbands and asked if they had time for us to explain the colors, and they said yes. The four girls stood in a circle with us as we went through the gospel. As we went through each verse, it became apparent which of them had a relationship with Jesus.

When we got to the blue verse we asked, "If you were standing at the gates of heaven and they asked, 'Why should we let you in?' what would you say?'"

The first girl answered, "Because I put my trust in Jesus." We went around the circle and most of them answered "Yeah, what she said."

At this point, the Lord put it on my heart to talk to one of the girls when she wasn't with the others. I felt an impression that she was ready to get saved. If it wasn't for that impression, I am not sure she had given enough clues for me to have figured it out on my own.

When we got to the last part where we ask if anyone wants to accept the gift, I knew that some of them had so I just asked if they hadn't already, would they like to. Three of them said they already had, but the girl the Lord put on my heart didn't respond. She stood there staring with her eyes open wide, but sort of trying to remain unnoticed. We thanked them for their time and the group was dismissed.

As this girl started to walk away, I asked her if she was with the others or if she had another minute or two. She said she was alone and could give us some extra time. I didn't really know how else to say it, so I just went for it. "You haven't ever done that before have you?"

"No," she responded.

"You're ready aren't you?"

She nodded.

All of a sudden I felt the Lord squeeze my insides. I didn't really have anything else on my mind, but I have learned over the years that when I get that feeling to just open my mouth and let the Lord speak through me.

What the Lord had me say was very personal, and as I spoke she started to tear up and told me that everything I was saying was true. We began to speak life into her, and she explained that all this Christianity stuff was new to her. She didn't grow up going to church, and the only reason she was even in Abilene was for college. She said that she had recently started attending a local church and that many of her questions were being dealt with even though she never told them to anyone.

Finally we asked her if she would like to pray to make Jesus her Lord, and she said yes. We walked her through our discipleship tab, where we explain the next steps. We asked if she would be interested in my teammate meeting with her on a regular basis to help her grow in the Lord, and she agreed! After a month or so had passed, I was informed that she had been baptized, that they had been meeting, and she was growing so fast!

Sometimes when you're in a crowd God will make someone stand out that you need to have a conversation with separately. It doesn't always mean they are going to be saved, you might just need to encourage them. In my story, I knew I needed to talk to this young lady apart from her friends, not because I thought she was being fake with us, but because she wasn't really opening up and I wanted her to be in a position where she could trust us.

There is a story in Luke 19 about a despised tax collector named Zacchaeus. He was super short and had a hard time seeing Jesus because the crowd was full of taller people, so he climbed a tree. No one knows how far away Jesus was or how long this guy was in the tree before Jesus noticed him, but at some point He does. Jesus had a whole crowd of people to choose from, and He chose to dine with Zacchaeus.

> But the people were displeased. "He has gone to be the guest of a notorious sinner," they grumbled.
> Meanwhile, Zacchaeus stood before the Lord and said, "I will give half my wealth to the poor, Lord, and if I have cheated people on their taxes, I will give them back four times as much!"
> Jesus responded, "Salvation has come to this home today, for this man has shown himself to be a true son of Abraham. For the Son of Man came to seek and save those who are lost." (Luke 19:7-10)

They are all still in front of the crowd when Jesus tells Zac that He's going to his house, and Zac says he's gonna make his wrongs right. I love this story because of how quickly Zac gets saved, it isn't this long, drawn out thing. Jesus gently invades his life and all of a sudden he's leaving his wicked ways. Jesus doesn't even call out his sin and say, "Hey there thiefy, I know you're robbing people and lining your pockets. You're selfish and you only think about yourself."

Just the mention of Jesus coming to his house causes conviction to sit on this guy and he starts repenting! Then just in case His disciples or critics forgot why He was on earth, Jesus wraps up with reminding everyone of the mission. "I am here to seek and save the lost." That means He was actively looking.

One of the most important things we need to learn from this story is to be looking for people. Don't just "people watch," but really look and ask the Lord to show you what He sees. More often than not we pass by people who are desperate for a touch from God and we're standing right there, but because we're so focused on what we're doing we miss them.

When you notice someone, ask the Lord if they are who you should be talking to. I know it's not popular to pick up people walking on the side of the road. I look for the ones who aren't asking for a ride, but are walking because they have to, especially when it is cold or rainy. Many times we miss them all together because we are not paying attention. Sometimes we talk ourselves out of talking to them.

Can you imagine this? Jesus stops and thinks about Zaccheaus. "Well…I know he has a reputation for taking more taxes than he should…so that means he's a thief. We'd better not stop for him, 'cause he could walk off with some of our money too."

Not only did Jesus see Zaccheaus, He got him off to the side. Jesus took the time to dine with him. For you, this could mean you're going to need to take someone out to eat, or have them to your house. I am personally okay with you inviting yourself to people's homes, although in our culture it may not go over well. But there are some people that will invite you over five minutes after meeting you and try to feed you!

Today let's take time to ask the Lord to open our eyes. Who are the Zacchaeus' at work? Who are the Zacchaeus' in my neighborhood? Who should I have a meal with? Who is lost that I need to find? Let's be intentional today to join Christ in His search for the lost.

RESPONSE

DAY 25
GARY, IN

SPIDER EARS

Before I go anywhere to share the gospel and pray for people, I always pray and ask the Lord where He wants me to go. This particular day, I kept seeing the train station/bus stop off of Broadway Avenue in my mind. I could not shake it, so I ran it by my team. I had been there a few years earlier, so I knew exactly where it was. My team agreed to try it out.

When we arrived, we walked around and prayed for a few people. A man that had gotten off the bus really stood out to me. When I caught up with him, he was standing beside the building in the smoking section. At the time I didn't have as much experience sharing the gospel, so I just asked him how I could pray for him. He said he didn't want me to pray for him, so I asked if I could at least join him while he was smoking. He nodded in agreement, so I stood there beside him while he blew smoke in my direction.

This man was incredibly tall, wearing a black leather jacket, and had tattoos all over. There were tattoos of spider webs all around his ears with spider tattoos made to look like they were crawling in and out of his ears. His head was shaved and tattooed as well. Without having a clue what to do, and not really wanting to offend the guy, I just stood there.

After a bit he asked me, "How were you baptized?"

I was confused. "Excuse me? It's pretty loud out here, with the trains and buses, I didn't understand you. What did you ask?"

"How were you baptized?" he asked me again, this time much clearer.

"With water? Sir, I really don't understand what you're asking."

"In what name were you baptized?" he asked.

"Uhh, the name of the Father, Son, and Holy Spirit."

"That's it!" he said. "You're not really saved! That's why I didn't want you to pray for me."

Everything inside of me was upset. He began telling me that he knew I wasn't saved because he used to be a preacher back in the day, until he got sick. When he got sick, he couldn't afford medicine so he drank to numb the pain. After a while, he was so addicted that he couldn't shake it. He lost his ministry, his wife, and kids, all to alcohol. As he spoke, my heart went out to the guy. I could feel the love of Jesus fill my heart, ceasing all the frustration from him telling me I wasn't saved.

He told me the only way you can baptize someone is in "Jesus' name" only, otherwise you're not saved. This time it didn't hurt. I loved him too much to let it bother me. This guy was running from the Lord with everything he had. The story of the prodigal son from Luke 15 ran through my head as this man divulged all of his theological expertise.

"How in the world can I speak into this guy?" I asked the Lord in my mind.

Right away, the Lord gave me a thought. This man had been lecturing me about the different beliefs his denomination had when I interrupted him. (I know our moms tell us that it's rude to interrupt, and I try not to do it, but it was necessary because the bus was going to leave at any moment and I did not want to miss out on an opportunity.)

"You need to get your oil," I said.

"What?" he questioned.

"You're out of oil, so you need to go get your oil."

"I don't understand," he said.

For the first time since I asked how I could pray for him, he gave me a opportunity to actually talk.

I explained that in Matthew, Jesus told a story about ten bridesmaids. Half of them used up their oil, and when the bridegroom came they weren't ready, so they had to run to the store which, in the end, made them miss out on the party. They couldn't get in because they didn't have their oil when they needed it.

"Do you remember that story?" I asked.

"Sort of," the man said.

"The point is this, man. Jesus is coming soon, and we don't have time to play games. Whether I am saved or not we both have to realize that we need to be ready when He returns."

Right then, the bus driver called out that it was time to go. The man grabbed his stuff and watched me as he walked to the bus. My heart broke. Here was a man trapped and bound by his vices, unable to set himself free. Here was a man who needed to know Jesus still loved him despite his spiritual adultery, and Jesus was calling him to come back.

If there is anything that drives me to share the gospel, it is this: soon Jesus will return, and I don't want to justify how I have spent my time. The last thing I want is for Him to confront me about how I had time to binge watch Netflix or the news, and never bothered to tell anyone about Him.

In Matthew 25, we see Jesus compare the Kingdom of heaven to some bridesmaids who are waiting for the groom to show up. There are ten bridesmaids in all, half of which are considered foolish, because they didn't bring extra oil with them. It turns out the groom seems to be running a bit later than expected so they all take a nap. While they are asleep, someone starts shouting that the groom is now on the way and the wedding is getting ready to begin.

Half of the ladies were ready to go right away because they were prepared and had brought along extra oil for their lamps. The other half had to run to their local convenience store to grab more oil, but by the time they got back, the wedding had already begun and they weren't let inside. In fact they stand there and yell,

> "'Lord! Lord! Open the door for us!'
> But he called back, 'Believe me, I don't know you!'
> So you, too, must keep watch! For you do not know the day
> or hour of my return." (Matthew 25:11-13)

Now I did some internet research for you, because to be honest these ladies don't make much sense, mostly because we have different wedding traditions than they did, and if we expect to understand anything Jesus said here then we need some help.

According to the Messianic Jewish Bible Society,* the ancient Jewish wedding had three stages: "shiddukhin (mutual commitment), erusin (engagement), and nissuin (marriage)."

Shiddukhin represents a time when the parents of the potential bride and groom or a matchmaker would negotiate the terms of the engagement. When it was settled, they would be immersed in water as a sign of spiritual cleansing and begin erusin.

A bride and groom would publicly enter a tiny tent called a huppa, the groom would give the bride something valuable, and they shared a cup of wine. This began a year long stage of "betrothal." The bride and the groom were officially married, but did not live together yet. The groom would go off to prepare their home, and she would get the furnishings together. At the end of erusin, the groom would return to his bride. They would have a parade as they returned to the home that was prepared.

Finally nissuin would take place. The groom would make a big deal over his bride, sometimes even carrying her back to the huppa, where they would have some wine and say some vows, and then consummate their marriage. Then there would be a party about seven days long where everyone would celebrate the wedding.

Now the important part to our story is the end of erusin. When the groom was ready, he would return to the bride's town, sometimes during the night, to take his bride home. Often the groom would be escorted by groomsmen who would carry torches on the way to the bride's house. One of the groomsmen would announce his coming, causing the bride and the bridesmaids to have to get up and around in a hurry in order to get ready.

Jesus' warning in this parable is to the ladies whose job it is to escort the bride. First He says they need to keep watch, because they don't know exactly when he is coming, but he is in fact coming. Next He is saying they need to be prepared, and in this particular case, the bridesmaids needed oil. Light would be necessary to return to the the father's house, as well as to join the feast. According to Jesus this feast was indoors, so if it was at night they would need oil to light the room. (I know this because I have Amish friends. Haha.)

There are many amazing things about this story that we could get into, but the part that is necessary to understand, and the point Jesus is trying to make, is that at some point in time the groom is going to return. When that day comes, the bridesmaids have to be ready to jump up and help the bride get her stuff together because it's time to go. As a bridesmaid you're not necessary for the marriage ceremony to start without you, so be ready. It's not about you, it's about the groom and his bride. However as a prepared bridesmaid, you get to join the bride and groom in a seven day party!

(WOMAN'S NOTE: "I can tell you that as a woman, and someone who works in the bridal business, if half of my bridesmaids were so underprepared that they missed part of my wedding, I'd have my groom tell them they couldn't come in too!" —Bea Wright, bridal seamstress extraordinaire, also an excellent tortilla maker, and most importantly…a woman.)

Today, the only thing I want you to consider is this. Are you ready for Christ's return? Are the people you love ready? Are your neighbors ready? Who do you know that is playing around, walking the fence, and not making up their mind?

Don't be a foolish bridesmaid. Be ready. If you're reading this book and you've fallen asleep because the bridegroom has been a long time in coming, wake up from your sleep! Be prudent. Go get your oil now, so that you don't get locked out of the banquet. Go! Tell your loved ones who have used up their oil to go get more.

For those of you who have been wise, even if you've fallen asleep, be ready at a moment's notice to jump up when the cry rings out. Tell everyone you know to get ready for Christ's return. He is coming soon.

*https://free.messianicbible.com/feature/ancient-jewish-wedding-customs-and-yeshuas-second-coming/

DAY 26
EAU CLAIRE, WI

THE DAY I GOT YELLED AT

I have been yelled at a few times on the street. Yet in all those encounters the people had made it pretty clear that they weren't mad at me. They were mad at the church. They were mad at the pastors who take advantage of little kids behind closed doors and the stupid power trips some of them have. And to be honest, those things make me want to make my own whip and start tossing tables. This time it was a bit different.

There were some guys that were heading straight from the lunch church to the evening church service because they had some "techie" stuff to get done for the service, so I hitched a ride with them. It was one of those days where a lot had been going on, and I really didn't want to go out on a team. I wasn't feeling well and just needed to rest.

Before we got to the church, someone had the idea to get coffee first. (Random fact you don't care about... I HATE coffee...but I do like smoothies.) Our vehicle was in the left lane, and all of a sudden the driver swerved across all lanes of traffic to turn right (sorry...we don't endorse that sort of bad driving) and said that the Lord told him to pray for the lady in the motel office on the corner. There were only three of us, and the other guy decided to go in with the driver to talk to the lady.

Figuring that three people might be a bit awkward, I decided to look for someone outside the office. There was a man smoking at the far end of the building, so I went to talk with him. Well, it was obvious after a few minutes that I was the last person he wanted to talk to, so I headed back toward the car.

As I looked around for someone else to pray for, I saw the building across the street. The sign stood out to me. There were cars in the parking lot and I could see people inside walking around and what looked like hanging out. It seemed as if it was a place I would fit in nicely so I headed over.

When I walked through the door, the man asked how he could help me. I told him I was new to the neighborhood, had never been there before, and figured I would stop in to check it out. So I asked, "What do you guys do here?"

He said, "...We sell cars."

I looked through the glass walls and felt like an idiot. "Ahhh, that's why there are cars everywhere in the parking lot. I just figured there were a lot of people here."

He definitely didn't like my response. "Are you interested in a car?"

I said, "Well, as much as I would love a new car, I can't afford one right now."

I felt like the biggest loser. It was clear he didn't want me there, but I didn't want to give up either. So I told him, "I'm with this thing called reviveWISCONSIN and that's why I'm in town. We're asking people in the community how we can pray for them."

The man yelled at me from his chair, "I'M AN ATHEIST, I DON'T PRAY!"

I told him, "That's okay, I'm a Christian and I will do the praying if you let me know what you'd like prayer for."

There was a girl on the other side of the entryway and she said she'd like prayer for good health, so I said, "How about this? I will pray for everyone over here that they have good health, and you sir, I will pray that you sell a lot of cars so that you can make a lot of money."

He yelled at me, "DON'T WASTE YOUR PRAYERS ON THAT!" (For someone who doesn't pray, he really seemed like an expert all of a sudden.)

"What would be a better use of my prayers?" I asked.

"PRAY FOR KIDS WITH CANCER OR SOMETHING LIKE THAT!"

So I replied, "How about this then? I will pray that all the people over here have good health and that all the kids in the hospitals with cancer would be healed, and that you, sir, would not sell any cars and that you don't make a lot of money. Is that what you want?"

"Yes!" He still yelled, but not as loudly this time.

Then his phone rang, and his whole attitude instantly changed. He became "Mr. Smooth" salesman and the lady on the other side of the door was typing on her computer with her head down as if to hide from Mr. Smooth. I stood there feeling like I was an inch tall. All I wanted to do was hide and cry. Everyone was busy so I decided to leave.

I put my hand on the door to take off and Mr. Smooth said, "Woah, woah, woah. I don't like what you're doing, but I admire your positivity."

I thanked him, blessed him, and left. Standing there on the street facing the building, you can literally see through the entire building because there are windows all the way around. I had managed to stand there with what felt like an idiotic smile on my face while a man screamed at me, and all I had wanted to do was hide.

When I got back to the motel where our car was parked, I was pretty sure it was locked so I sat on a bench. But of course, there was Mr. Smooth sitting at his desk still looking right at me through those big windows. And there I was, across the street and still unable to escape him.

I tried to look around and pretend I was unfazed by him, when all of a sudden the door beside my bench opened, and a guy came out and leaned against the wall. He started to talk to me, and after a bit I asked how I could pray for him. He let me pray, and when I gave him the wristband he gladly wanted to go through it. Knowing Mr. Smooth was still across the street watching me, I tried to keep my body language in check. While I was walking the man through the scriptures, it was everything I could do to make sure that I didn't look like I was forcing anything on him. I was praying that the Lord would speak to Mr. Smooth the entire time I was with the other guy. Another soul was brought into the Kingdom of heaven that day while Mr. Smooth watched the entire thing across the street.

The truth about this story for me is that even though a man gave his life to Jesus that day, the encounter with Mr. Smooth hurt. In Matthew 5:11 Jesus says, "God blesses you when people mock you and persecute you and lie about you and say all sorts of evil things against you because you are my followers."

I know this passage shows me that I am blessed because of that experience, but that doesn't mean it didn't suck. There are many reasons why it was less than awesome. I hate not being able to turn a person around. It bothers me that when I walked away from the encounter, that man chose hell. It also bothers me that he yelled at me. Sure I kept a smile on my face, and I guess I kept my cool, but I felt like the biggest loser in the world.

My problem here is that I compare myself to others who would have done a better job at sharing the gospel than I do, and even though I know I shouldn't compare, I still do it. I am not superhuman, and even though I call myself a superhero, the truth is I don't have it all together. I make mistakes, I get offended when I shouldn't, and I deal with emotions. Just because you're blessed doesn't mean life will be easy. However, just because something is hard, that doesn't mean it isn't worth doing.

When I saw my wife later that day, she asked me if I actually prayed that Mr. Smooth wouldn't sell any cars. I felt it wasn't "the Christian thing" to do. She told me that he gave me permission to pray that he doesn't sell any cars or make a lot of money, so I should pray for that.

She then explained that maybe God would use that in his life to bring about his repentance. Maybe he would remember the day he rejected me, and be able to track his inability to sell cars to my prayer and turn to the Lord. I realized that my wife was right (again). So we prayed together exactly what I had said to the man, that he wouldn't sell any cars and wouldn't make any money.

Today as you leave your porcelain throne, or before you go to work, or before you go to sleep, ask the Lord this: is there someone I need to share the gospel with today? Is there someone I haven't spoken to because I am afraid of the way they would respond? Is there an angry car salesman that I need to visit? We need to overcome our fear of men by fearing God alone. Let's call ourselves blessed when people speak evil of us for following Jesus. It's okay if people think we're weird. We are!

DAY 27
ABILENE, TX

I DIDN'T SAY ANYTHING INTELLIGENT

Let me start today off by telling this quick side story before the real story. I had the honor of speaking at a church in the Dallas/Fort Worth area on my way home from Abilene. The story I am about to share was told during that service and my wife, who was listening in the back, told me afterwards, "That story was not very exciting, why did you share that?"

I told her about a conversation I had after the service while I was greeting people. This lady walked up and said, "Hey, you know that story about the shoe store?"

"Yeah?"

"You didn't say anything intelligent."

I couldn't help but laugh. It was so incredibly true. I am far from intelligent, but that's the beauty of what happens when I am intentional about sharing the gospel. It's obvious that God shows up.

"I go to the shoe store," she said. "I could pray with the woman behind the counter!"

She then proceeded to tell me about how when we had been in the area the year before, she had come to all the testimony times. When she heard the stories she would think to herself that she wasn't as bold as the guy in that story, or doesn't have faith like the girl in this other story. She would listen and think that she couldn't evangelize like we do. But because of the shoe store story (that I am about to tell you), she realized that she could indeed share her faith. She told me she would be at the next outreach to go out on a team.

Now, on to the greatly anticipated, most likely uninteresting story that you have been wanting to read instead of what you are currently reading.

It was the first day of outreach in Abilene and my team ended up being three college-aged ladies and myself. We had been to a few places and prayed for a few people and it was getting close to the time we needed to wrap up to check in at the church (it's a way our ministry makes sure everyone is safe).

We drove by a shoe store and joked about how girls can always use a new pair of shoes. The girl that was driving mentioned that she could use a scrunchie. (Because I have a wife, two daughters and three sisters I knew what that was.) We went in and the place was pretty much empty except for the girl behind the counter.

My team walked up, and the ladies were very bold. They purchased the scrunchie, and as our driver was getting her change, she asked how we could pray for the cashier, a 19-year-old girl. She said she'd like prayer for her boyfriend who was deployed and she wanted him to return home unharmed. The girls on my team prayed for her and when they were done we offered her a wristband. We asked if she had a minute so we could explain the colors. We didn't want her to get into trouble for socializing instead of working. The store was empty and she said that because we were the only people there, it was her job to entertain us.

We went through the scriptures with her and found out that even though she lived in the Bible Belt, she had never in her life read the Bible. She had never been told that Jesus loved her. She knew that Jesus was crucified on a cross, but that was it. She had never heard that He rose again after being dead for three days.

We asked if she believed in her heart that Jesus was alive, and if she would like to make him her Lord. We explained that if she did, then Jesus would have the right to tell her how to spend her money, how to treat her parents, and how to relate to her boyfriend. She said yes, that she wanted to do it. One of the girls had her repeat a salvation prayer.

Afterward, we asked if she would be interested in having someone meet with her to talk to her more about how to follow Jesus, and that the girls on my team would love to do that. She was excited for that, and as we got her information, it turned out that all four ladies were in the same class at their university, but for some reason they had never met.

This is a very simple story. A woman had a group of people come in to her work and call out to her to come follow Jesus. Barely knowing anything about Jesus, she took a step and put her life in His hands. There were no fireworks, or disco balls, or loud instruments to declare what happened, but it was real, and it is part of her story. In the scriptures there are similar stories of people who were at work when they decided to follow Christ, so let's examine one in particular.

> One day as Jesus was walking along the shore of the Sea of Galilee, He saw two brothers—Simon, also called Peter, and Andrew—throwing a net into the water, for they fished for a living. Jesus called out to them, "Come, follow me, and I will show you how to fish for people!" And they left their nets at once and followed Him. (Matt. 4:18-20)

Here, we see two brothers working at the family business, when Jesus shows up. The most important part of this whole thing is that when Jesus shows up, we respond. Jesus was walking through their neighborhood when He saw Peter and Andrew.

In the same way, we are called to go out and walk by those who need Jesus. These guys were at work. They were busy. It wasn't like Jesus met them at the local coffee shop or at a park, while they were sitting around waiting for something to do. If their dad was anything like my dad, they probably had to work hard, just to keep up. But then, Jesus showed up and called out, "Follow me."

Didn't Jesus know they were busy? Didn't Jesus know they were trying to make a living here? "But I have a family to feed," would have been going through my mind if I was Peter.

Then Jesus uses language they understand. "I'll show you how to fish for people." Another way of saying that is, "Hey, come work for me." Something compelled them enough to drop what they were doing and follow Him.

Now we didn't tell the girl in our story to quit her job at the shoe store and follow us, but I believe for some people that really is the case...that's literally what I did. I believe that there are times when Jesus calls you to step out and trust Him for absolutely everything, and follow Him. I believe that Peter and Andrew didn't have a single regret for for leaving everything to follow Jesus. Both of them became mighty men of God, eventually becoming key leaders in the body of Christ. They even end up becoming martyrs years later. You never know who you might call out that is one day going to shape the world.

The process of sharing the gospel and making disciples is simple. Even when it is intense it is still simple. Today as you go about your day, take some time to talk to the one in front of you. Maybe you too will be at a shoe store. Buy some shoes and ask how you can pray. Maybe you're buying lumber to work on your house, why not ask them how you can pray for them before you leave the store? Keep your eyes open, and talk to the people that are where you are. Call out to them, "Come follow me," and when they do, just lead them straight to Jesus.

RESPONSE

DAY 28
GOSHEN, IN

NOW THAT'S A LOT OF CATS!

Every once in a while the Lord allows me to have a vision. This particular night while my team prayed, I saw a green house. It was as if I was looking up at it. There was a window, and I could tell it was a second story window because there were shingles underneath. It seemed as if I was only looking at part of the house, because I couldn't see the majority of it, just from the window on over.

Anytime I see something like that I write it down, because you never know if it will turn up or not. My teammate Floyd said that he saw a wooden park bench, with the seat back going side to side instead of up and down. Then my other teammate, Ken, said he heard the word "park." So we wrote both of those down too.

As we discussed where we should go, we obviously knew we should start with a park. There was a park within walking distance of us, but we didn't know if there were any houses that bordered it. The city of Goshen has public benches, but they're all made of metal and the seat backs go up and down and not side to side.

We figured we should head to that park anyway to see what we could find. As we neared the entryway, I saw a green house that was next to the park. We decided to get closer and see if anyone was home. As we walked, I couldn't help but notice that on the west side of the street, there were four or five cats wrestling and playing.

"Wow, that's a lot of cats!" I said.

There was a house directly across the street from the cats that had another bunch of cats! They were everywhere. On the porch, on cars, crawling all over everything. We got closer, talking about all the cats, when we heard this guy from behind the house yell, "It's because she feeds them!"

"What?" I yelled back. I hadn't heard him very well, so we kept walking toward him to hear better.

He hobbled closer and said again, "It's because she feeds them! Sometimes you will even see raccoons eating with all them cats."

"Oh wow!" I said. "I've never seen that many cats in one place before."

"You should see the place when the food comes out!" he said.

We talked about the cat lady for a little bit longer, and he asked us what brought us to this part of town.

"Well, we are out in the neighborhood asking people how we can pray for them. Is there anything we can pray for you for?" I said.

"Absolutely! I fell off the roof and I broke my foot!" he said, pointing to his foot, which was all swollen and mangled. He told us he didn't have any insurance, and he didn't have a job after he injured his back at work, so now he was waiting for workers' comp to approve his procedures.

"Would it be okay if we prayed for healing in your foot and back?" we asked.

"Sure," he replied.

Floyd put his hand on the man's foot, and I put my hand on his shoulder, after he gave us permission. We commanded healing in Jesus' name, that all pain would leave his body, and that he would be totally and completely whole. When we finished praying, he said his back was feeling better, but his foot still looked awful.

"I used to go to church," he said, "but I got out of it. I think the Lord brought you two here to remind me that I should be going."

"That very well could be," we said. "Would you like one of these wristbands to remind you that we prayed?"

He got really excited. His daughter, who had been watching from a distance, came running over.

"I want a wristband," she said.

We gave her one and asked if she would like to know what the colors mean. She was very excited, and began to tell us about how she had seen those Bibles before. Back in 2015 her mom had gone to the reviveINDIANA services, and she had wanted a Bible ever since. We walked the two of them through the verses, and she said she had never heard them before. Her dad said that he hadn't been to church in a really long time, and he wanted her to make up her own mind about what she believes.

We asked her if she would want to place her trust in Jesus by accepting the gift of salvation and she said, "YES!"

We prayed with her and went through the discipleship tab with them. She said she was going to be living far away and that she would find someone to pour into her there. The man said that he would like to be discipled as well. His life was a mess and his wife and kids were living somewhere else. As it was, he was homeless and staying with friends. We asked him who he wanted to disciple him, and he picked Floyd.

As we turned to leave, I looked across the street, and there was the exact view of the green house that I had written down.

I said, "Floyd! There's the house!"

He said, "Jesse! There's the bench!"

Here was the bench, right beside where we were talking with this man and his daughter the entire time. I explained what we were talking about to the man and showed him my phone where I had it all written down, and his mouth dropped!

"You mean, the Lord specifically sent you guys to us tonight!" he said. "Wow. It blows my mind that He would care that much."

After we left, Floyd and I kept up with him. Every time we've talked, this man has told me that that night changed his life. Floyd has been pouring into him. It has had its challenges, but discipleship always does.

Let's read a story where something similar happens.

> Now there was a believer in Damascus named Ananias. The
> Lord spoke to him in a vision, calling, "Ananias!"
> "Yes, Lord!" he replied.
> The Lord said, "Go over to Straight Street, to the house of
> Judas. When you get there, ask for a man from Tarsus named
> Saul. He is praying to me right now. I have shown him a
> vision of a man named Ananias coming in and laying hands
> on him so he can see again." (Acts 9:10-12)

It goes on to say that Ananias argues with the Lord about whether or not it's a good idea for him to go pray for this man, Saul, who has been murdering Christians. The Lord convinces him that he should, so Ananias goes and does exactly as he's told.

I love this story. I love that Jesus shows up to a guy in a vision to tell him to talk to someone he is scared to talk to. Jesus gives him a specific person, at a specific location, and even tells him what's wrong with him and what he's supposed to do about it. Jesus also lets him know that this man will suffer for His name. All that happens in a vision.

> Then, after doing all those things,
> I will pour out my Spirit upon all people.
> Your sons and daughters will prophesy.
> Your old men will dream dreams,
> and your young men will see visions.
> In those days I will pour out my Spirit
> even on servants—men and women alike. (Joel 2:28-29)

The vision I saw was specific to us, to confirm that we were right where we needed to be. And if we hadn't been looking for the green house and the bench we could have ended up somewhere else at the park, or not even at the park at all. Be discerning when people tell you they've heard from God, but also be open to the reality that maybe they did. There is a 50/50 chance. Test it and see if your spirit agrees.

As you read this story today, you might be saying to yourself, "Man, I have never seen a vision." Don't think that there is anything wrong with you. Before I knew that God could and would use my imagination to speak to me, and that I didn't have to rely on feeling like my heart was going to explode before I did something, I thought I didn't have them. In fact, when I realized the Lord was speaking to me that way, I repented because I knew that the Lord had been doing it all along, but I had been ignoring it, because I wasn't told to pay attention to it.

Today, ask the Lord to give you specific instructions. Ask Him to speak to you in a way you can understand. I want you to share the gospel, but ultimately what you really need is to know what Jesus is saying to you for yourself. How cool would it be if the Lord showed you something today and you were able to lead someone to Jesus because you acted on it? Give it a try.

DAY 29
RICHMOND, IN

DEMONSTRATE THE POWER

Sometimes I have the privilege to speak at the churches prior to the Revive outreach week to try and create some momentum. My family wasn't able to come with me on this trip because I would be in the car for six hours so that I could be at the church for roughly three hours. It's just too much for little kids to do in a day, so my brother-in-law went with me.

The Lord had been heavily dealing with me on the idea that there should be a demonstration of power as well as the gospel going forth. Up to this point, I had shared the gospel quite a bit and had seen a number of people saved, but I hadn't really seen the power of God show up like it did in the New Testament. I had been praying for miracles, signs and wonders, and healings for years. Every once in a while someone would get healed, but I haven't always gotten the results I've wanted or hoped for.

During worship one night the band played a song that went along with the message that was on my heart. This song says that because the Spirit of God was present, a miracle could take place. Immediately the Lord told me He wanted to demonstrate His power that night.

With all confidence that God was going to heal someone, I took the microphone. I began to preach the message. I was excited because I knew in my gut that God was going to back up the message with power. I was teaching from Acts 3 about how Peter and John were walking on their way to church when they saw a cripple. The man asked them for money, Peter said he didn't have any, but he'd share what he did have. In verse 6 Peter says, "In the name of Jesus Christ the Nazarene, get up and walk!" At that moment the crippled man stood up and walked!

I said, "Tonight the Lord wants to demonstrate His power for you. The Lord wants to back up the preaching of His word. Who here is sick?" I scanned the audience. Nobody was saying anything. I said again, "Who needs a healing?"

A girl all the way to the far right of the room said, "I do." She had crutches with her.

I asked her what was wrong and she told everyone that she was in a lot of pain and explained the injury. I told the students sitting around her to put their hands on her. One girl put her hands directly on the injury. Then I told them to command healing in her body, in Jesus' name. The whole room started to pray for her.

The girl immediately got up without her crutches and began to shout, "I'M HEALED! I'M HEALED! I'M HEALED!"

She began to run back and forth, jumping, as we all clapped. She was so excited that even after we continued with the message, she kept running back and forth in the corner of the room. After the service her mom came up to me, thanked me for praying, and confirmed the pain that her daughter had been in. She told us that it really was a miracle that she didn't need the crutches anymore.

Jesus called His twelve disciples together and gave them authority to cast out evil spirits and to heal every kind of disease and illness. (Matt. 10:1)

I love this passage, because Jesus is literally getting ready to do what we are talking about in this book. He is sending them out in teams of two. Jesus believed that because He gave them the order to go and heal an illness, that those illnesses would be healed.

We as Christians should expect that people will be healed when we pray. Do I think it will happen every time? I don't think it's my job to worry about that or to try to manufacture a healing or a miracle. According to Jesus, my job is to cast out evil spirits and to heal sicknesses and diseases. (Some of you are freaking out right now because you see that it is saying to cast out evil spirits. Part of the Kingdom of God advancing on the earth means going beyond what you're used to, to find others who are bound by evil spirits.)

Oh, but there's more. If we keep reading He gives more details for us.

> Go and announce to them that the Kingdom of Heaven is near. Heal the sick, raise the dead, cure those with leprosy, and cast out demons. Give as freely as you have received! (Matt. 10: 7-8)

Now let's look at each of these commands in detail.

"Announce." The disciples have been given an incredible message, "the Kingdom of Heaven is near." We need to identify the lost and proclaim this message.

"Heal." We have been given permission by Jesus to touch or pray for those who are sick, and because of who we are in Him, having been clothed in His righteousness and given the authority, that person will get well. I need to get to a place where I can believe that people will be healed because of Jesus being with me and in me.

Practically this might mean that while you're out shopping for your next book and you see a person in the corner of the room with a cast on, you can be confident enough in the Lord to go over there and offer to pray. Maybe they say no, but maybe they say yes. What if they don't get healed? Well, at least it won't be because you didn't try. And what if they are healed? Jesus gets the glory.

"Raise." It is much more fluffy and likely to make people feel good to say that Jesus is referring here to those who are spiritually dead. Sure. It may mean that a tiny bit, but what He is really saying here is that we as disciples of Jesus should "raise the dead."

The truth is that for most of us, because we don't see this on a regular basis, we either don't believe it will happen for us, or we try to put limitations on it. Raising the dead is never going to have a social norm to follow, unless we tap into the social norms of heaven. If we are honest, there is not a single time in scripture where someone gets raised from the dead and it is a "normal" situation.

Jesus yells at a buried dead guy, and he comes out of his grave (John 11:43-44). When Jesus died on the cross it says that saints were raised from the dead, having come out of their tombs (Matt. 27:52-53). Elijah and Elisha both had to lay down on top of a kid (1 Kings 17:21, 2 Kings 4:34-35). Talk about socially awkward!

These passages have all kinds of potential for us to look bad. Raising the dead does not make sense in everyday life. I can't explain exactly how to make a miracle happen, except to be like Jesus. If someone comes to you, expecting you to do something because you're the "man of God," then listen to God and do what He tells you.

"Cure." This goes along with healing the sick in some ways, because any ailment would require healing, but the issue of leprosy is so much deeper, not on a physical or molecular level, but emotionally and spiritually. In Leviticus 13 we see that,

> Those who suffer from a serious skin disease must tear their clothing and leave their hair uncombed. They must cover their mouth and call out, "Unclean! Unclean!" As long as the serious disease lasts, they will be ceremonially unclean. They must live in isolation in their place outside the camp. (vv. 45-46)

Over time this created a massive disconnect, because lepers weren't able to come into the city. They were the outcasts. In order to obey the command from Jesus you would have to risk your own health, causing you to value the other person even more than yourself. Curing the lepers would also restore people to society, giving them dignity in some ways, and allowing them to go back to work, and participate in the sacrifices again. This means they would be able to enjoy the presence of God, and the benefits that come from that.

This may mean that you're going to have to lay hands to pray for someone who physically won't be appealing. They may smell bad or have open wounds that won't be pretty to look at. There is a good chance you won't find these people at your local country club or golf course. You may need to make up your mind in advance that no matter how awful the disease may seem, they are still loved by you and their heavenly Father. Again, you have the power to speak or to lay hands on those afflicted with skin diseases and cure them.

"Cast." As if the rest of this passage isn't controversial enough, let's add something about demons. There are a lot of Christians out there who do not believe that this is an issue in America. The truth is, people who are demon possessed have often been handed over to the health care system instead of to the church. They are diagnosed, medicated, and locked up to keep them away from the public. In some ways we should be thankful, because it allows our children to be safer, but in other ways we as Christians need to be aware that this command is still for today.

Practically it is really simple. The way Jesus did it was by commanding the evil spirits to come out. Here are a few examples.

Then Jesus rebuked the demon in the boy, and it left him. From that moment the boy was well. (Matt. 17:18)

Suddenly, a man in the synagogue who was possessed by an evil spirit cried out... But Jesus reprimanded him. "Be quiet! Come out of the man," he ordered. (Mark 1:23; 25)

When Jesus saw that the crowd of onlookers was growing, he rebuked the evil spirit..."I command you to come out of this child and never enter him again!" (Mark 9:25)

For Jesus had already commanded the evil spirit to come out of him. (Luke 8:29)

There are some things that happen in each encounter that are unique from each other, causing Jesus and the disciples to interact differently each time. Sometimes people were throwing themselves into a fire (Matthew 17:15), or foaming out the mouth (Mark 9:20), or they're deaf and mute (Mark 9:25), or they're breaking chains and shackles (Luke 8:29). The thing that was always consistent is that Jesus didn't leave those people possessed.

Practically speaking, most of the encounters that Jesus had with demons, and the ones the disciples had as well, were pretty intense and could cause you to be afraid. Those who are demon possessed tend to behave abnormally, which causes us to naturally want to leave them alone. I'd like to encourage you in the moment when you discern that you're in the presence of a "demoniac" (for lack of a better term), to ask the Lord if He wants you to intervene. He can see if it is mental illness or a demon, as well as the rest of the ins and outs of the situation. If the Lord gives you the go ahead, step up and rebuke it in Jesus' name.

Your heart should be that the Lord would show up in the situations around us to prove His greatness so that people will respond to the message of the gospel, as well as that we would be close to Him in more than just our actions. Today before we go looking for God to show up in other people's lives, let's first examine our hearts. Then let's look for people who may need God to show up in this way.

If you don't know where to go to find people who have physical ailments that need healed, try a college campus. There are always athletes who have been hurt and want to get better so they can get back into the game. Look for people in wheelchairs or crutches, or that are coughing, and politely say something like, "Hey, this might sound really strange, but I was wondering if I could pray for you?" Then pray if they say yes.

There are people who will NOT want to be healed. It may seem strange, but some people are more fearful of losing their disability (which means having to get a job because they'll lose that money) than they are excited for healing. Bless them and move on. We are looking for people who want to be healed.

If you are new to this, don't make it complicated. Pray short, concise, faith-filled prayers. Leave the results to God. Let Him back up His name. I highly recommend that you ask for permission to lay your hand on the person wherever the pain or problem is. After you pray, ask them if it's better. If it is, have them verify it by going to the doctor. If it isn't better, that's okay, don't give up. Sometimes the Lord tests our willingness to obey Him even when it doesn't make sense. Keep praying.

RESPONSE

DAY 30
KOKOMO, IN/BLOOMINGTON, IN/CHICAGO, IL

MY SOUL LAID BARE

When I first started out sharing the gospel through the Time to Revive method, I had only ever known how to do it from a pulpit. I had lead a number of people to the Lord when I was a youth pastor and had been privileged enough to baptize a few too. However, when I started hitting the streets with Revive, it took a long time for me to see any fruit. Even then, it took a long time for me to see fruit consistently.

I was in Kokomo, Indiana and there was a man from where I lived who was baptizing a person from Kokomo that he had led to the Lord that day. I will be honest, I should have been thrilled, but I was more jealous than anything.

"Why is it that everywhere he goes, he's baptizing people left and right? I am so much better with people than he is," I thought to myself.

Soon after, in Bloomington, Indiana while I was helping with reviveKIDS, I watched a girl walk into the building and right up to this guy. The next thing I know, he's leading her through the Bible and band, and she's giving her life to Christ! Again, instead of being thrilled that someone was saved, I was filled with jealousy.

I began to ask the Lord, "What is inside of me that is preventing me from leading people to You, like this guy? I know You called me to do this, but it seems as if I am missing something."

That day I even asked the man, "What are you doing that I'm not doing?"

He said, "I don't know... They just come to me."

He was absolutely humble. He never rubbed it in, he never shamed me, and yet for some reason, in my heart I was jealous.

At Revive we teach how to practically love people, whether you need to mow someone's grass, or help them pull weeds, or buy a meal. Whatever it looks like to shower that person your with love, do it. I began to ask myself, in city after city, "What does love really look like?"

One night I found myself in 1 Corinthians 13, well known for being the "love" chapter. The first three verses read like this,

> If I could speak all the languages of earth and of angels, but didn't love others, I would only be a noisy gong or a clanging cymbal. If I had the gift of prophecy, and if I understood all of God's secret plans and possessed all knowledge, and if I had such faith that I could move mountains, but didn't love others, I would be nothing. If I gave everything I have to the poor and even sacrificed my body, I could boast about it; but if I didn't love others I would have gained nothing.

As I read these verses, I began to feel that double-edged sword that cuts through bone and marrow (Heb. 4:12) working its way into my heart. The reality is this: I gained nothing. I was nothing. This passage is explicitly clear. If you do not have love, you are just a bunch of noise.

Over the course of those first several months with Revive, I realized that I loved to hit the streets. I loved every bit of it. I loved to share the gospel. Even though I didn't lead tons of people to the Lord, I loved to do it. As that sword dug deep into my heart, I saw that, really, I loved myself. I didn't go out for the sake of the lost. I wasn't staying up at night because of a burden to see less people in hell. I was only out for myself. Selfishness had riddled me.

Love is patient and kind. Love is not jealous or boastful or proud or rude. It does not demand its own way. It is not irritable, and it keeps no record of being wronged. It does not rejoice about injustice but rejoices whenever the truth wins out. Love never gives up, never loses faith, is always hopeful and endures through every circumstance. (1 Cor. 13:4-7)

There I was, filled with jealousy, because there was someone leading more people to Jesus than me and I thought I should be way more effective than he was. My focus wasn't on others, it was only on myself. This change took place in my heart over a long period of seven months. It didn't just happened all at once.

But I remember that as I started to lay myself down at Jesus' feet, the more I cared about the lost. As I would repent for being full of myself, the more the Lord would fill me with His love for those around me that had made me jealous. Where I watched in jealousy, now I watch in amazement of how incredibly gracious the Lord is to allow me to see lives changed for the glory of God. When I am honest with myself, the more I recognize the lack of fruit, the more I see the lack of humility and abounding selfishness inside me.

1 Corinthians 13:8 says "Love never fails" (NASB). For far too long I measured my worth or success by how many people I led to the Lord, which is crazy, because at that time I wasn't leading anyone to the Lord. I was excited to pray for people, but I wasn't measuring the success of my encounters by asking myself if I loved that person well. Did I do or say something to help them know they are loved? Or did I only do and say things that I hoped would have amazing results?

Matthew 3:8 says to "bear fruit in keeping with repentance" (NASB). For two years this passage has been echoing through my heart as the Lord has exposed the junk in my life. It is so easy to slip into this self-righteous mindset that allows you to think that because you're a child of God, you no longer need to pay attention to your sin. That's not true, but it happens nonetheless.

I went to Chicago, Illinois for a test run to see if Revive would work. There is a man there named Marlon, whom I had the honor to serve with on the streets. We only went out one time together, and it forever changed my life.

We walked up to a girl who was leaning up against a bus stop sign, and Marlon said in his amazing spanish accent, "We are with a group of believers in the community, can we pray for you?"

I noticed he wasn't asking how he could pray, just whether or not he could pray. She nodded her head, and he lifted one hand to heaven and said, "Father, in Jesus' name," and BAM. He had a word of knowledge.

"You don't know your parents do you?" he asked.

"No," she said, "I was raised by my relatives."

Marlon started to speak into her. Just one thing after another, after another. He spoke for maybe two or three minutes straight, and this girl was just bawling. Finally he said, "Are you ready to get saved?"

"Yes!" she said.

Right there, he led her through a sinner's prayer as she wiped tears from her eyes.

Afterward he introduced us and said, "Jesse here would like to explain to you what just happened."

I was shocked and overwhelmed! I had seen stuff like that in services before, but never when I was on the street. Not like that. What she had been told was specific and detailed. It's truth penetrated her heart and she clearly saw that God loved her. All I could think was "Wow!"

I asked the Lord, "Show me...what do I need to do to be that effective? What is inside of me that is getting in the way of people encountering Jesus in a way that changes their lives forever?"

As I searched the Word, Matthew 3:8 was right there. When I read it, it jumped out at me and choked me. It was as if the Lord said, "You want to produce a lot of fruit in my kingdom? This is what it takes. Repentance. And it isn't this one and done deal, you have to live a lifestyle of continuous repentance."

Don't just take the easy way out, let the Holy Spirit use the Word of God to cut into the deepest parts of yourself and pull out the junk. Let the Spirit do a deep clean. The more I have repented of my pride, and jealousy, and my selfish ambition, the more and more fruit I have seen.

Today as you read this, ask the Lord to show you what it is that is preventing you from seeing continuous fruit, not just in terms of your own character, which is good too, but in terms of souls being saved. I believe that a huge portion of why we don't see revival in America is that we are so full of ourselves that we don't have room for Jesus.

"Father, what's inside of me that prevents me from seeing fruit like I should be?" Allow Him to speak to your heart. If there is something that immediately comes to mind and it makes your heart race, there is a really good chance you should repent of that. Today before you leave the house, get right before the Lord and shift your focus from yourself to Jesus, and to introducing people to Him.

DAY 31
CHICAGO, IL

SO THE PARTY BEGAN

WARNING THIS CHAPTER IS SEVERELY LONGER THAN THE REST. READ AT YOUR OWN RISK. READING MAY CAUSE YOUR EYEBALLS TO FALL OUT. IF YOUR EYEBALLS DO FALL OUT, DON'T SAY YOU WEREN'T WARNED.

This story took place over the same time period as the one from Chicago that I shared on Day 30. Let me begin by saying that I am really hesitant to share this story, because at times I get so frustrated with my own heart. I judge people when I shouldn't. I don't love well like I need to, but because I believe this story will encourage you to be more like Jesus, and not like me, I will share it.

My friend Scott Troyer and I ended up on a team together. I had to use the toilet, and the closest one that wasn't a Porta John was at the Dunkin' Donuts up the street, about a tenth of a mile or so. We went in and while I was in the bathroom, Scott got in line. When I came out there was a young man standing next to Scott.

"Are you die-hard or bandwagon?" he asked us.

"Uhh… What do you mean?" we asked.

"You know. Are you die hard fans or bandwagon fans?" he said as he pointed to Scott's Cubs shirt.

We stood there, caught off guard, and before we could respond he said, "You must be bandwagon then."

Personally I don't even like the Cubs…really I don't pay attention to sports at all (but I didn't think it necessary to share that part with him). He began talking to us. He had tattoos all over. His head was shaved, except for a tiny mohawk, and had a huge scar on the side. He wore sunglasses inside, and just about everything out of his mouth was derogatory.

I joked with him about how I am Mexican and he said, "You know, there is a really great Mexican restaurant right there!" And he pointed toward it.

To be absolutely honest, I think both Scott and I sort of wished we could move on because he was so opinionated, it was hard to be around him. He talked a lot and it was just really difficult, but when he pointed to the restaurant, I got the hint.

"Would you like to join us for some salsa and chips or something?" I asked.

"Man, I would love to. I just have to drop off this drink for my dad first," he said.

We walked with him to his house, which was right across the street, and then over to the restaurant. We joked when we got inside because everything was in Spanish, and I don't speak Spanish even though I really am half-Mexican. Everyone thought I knew how to read the menu, but I didn't.

We ordered the chips and salsa and for about two hours, we listened as this guy rambled on and on. We talked about just about everything. Finally we asked how we could pray for him. He told us he's not really religious, but he had been to church a few times. He didn't really want to keep going because he just wanted to be selfish. He told us about how he had been hit by a car when he was a kid, so he was on disability for life. He showed us the scar, which went along the side of his head, adding to his skinhead look.

We prayed for him and then he let us walk him through the Bible. At the end of the verses, he told us the same thing. He wasn't really into religion because he wanted to be able to do whatever he wanted, like party at the Cubs games. He knew that his life was full of things that if he gave himself over to Jesus, he wouldn't be able to do anymore. After a while we said our goodbyes and headed back to the tent, which served as our home base.

The next day the team I was on wanted to go a direction that would require us to go right beside this guy's house. I tried to convince them to go a different way because he had told us that he sits on his steps a lot. Something inside of me knew that he would be on his steps and I didn't want to spend another whole afternoon with an angry guy who didn't want to get saved. I wanted to be out where people knew they were lost and wanted to be found, not with this guy who only wanted to hang out and eat our chips and salsa. My team was convinced that we were supposed to go in that direction despite my subtle attempts to take us elsewhere.

Sure enough, we came walking by and there he was sitting on his steps. He saw me, threw his hands in the air, and yelled, "Jesse!"

I felt bad, but I was not excited at all. It was the last place I wanted to be. I asked the Lord how in the world I could get around spending another afternoon with this guy who didn't want to get saved. I had an idea.

"Hey man! Do you know of anyone in your neighborhood who could use prayer?"

He thought about it and said, "Yeah, my next door neighbor."

We went to their house and they let us in, and of course selfish Mr. Cubs Fan came along. At first I was really frustrated that he did, but he sat on the couch quietly and respectfully and just hung out. I was surprised. When we were done praying, he went home.

"Well, that wasn't as bad as I expected," I thought to myself.

The following day I was in a meeting at Dunkin' Donuts. I have a required weekly Zoom call, which I can do from my phone, but I needed wifi…which of course was only at Dunkin' Donuts. While I was in my meeting, I heard a pounding on the window beside me! There was Mr. Cubs Fan again, excited to see me.

He came into the store and I told him "Man, I am in a meeting, but if you want to meet me at the tent I should be there after a bit."

He left the store and when I got to the tent, he was there hanging out with the Mexican ladies that were getting dinner around. He was having fun, talking with them and sampling all the food.

That night he stayed for the service. In Chicago, all the services were in Spanish because the all churches that had invited us were Hispanic. They translated the messages, but there was an amazing Latin feel. Mr. Cubs Fan sat in the front row on the opposite side of the tent as me.

After the service, he came up to me and said, "I don't know if it was the music, or the Lord, but during the music I felt something cover me from head to toe."

I said, "Well, did you ask Him?"

"Huh?" he responded.

"Did you ask the Lord, 'Was that You or the music?'"

"Oh." He walked over to where he had been sitting.

I watched as he sat there talking to himself with his hands, then stood up, shrugged his shoulders and walked out of the tent. Well, now I wanted to know! This guy I didn't really want to be around, was growing on me. I wanted to know what had covered him from head to toe.

Mr. Cubs Fan showed up bright and early the next morning. He asked if he could join us on teams. I said, "…You do know you don't have to go right? You aren't technically a Christian remember? You wanted to be selfish."

"Yeah, I know, I just wanna hang out."

"Well, if you promise you won't interrupt anything, or distract us from praying with people, then I guess you can come along."

He joined my team, and was polite and courteous the entire time. In fact he just stood there quietly while we led a guy to the Lord. I was so confused. That night, I had to head home before the service started, but the local group had decided to keep going for twenty-one days.

The next day I had a friend request on Facebook from Mr. Cubs Fan. I accepted, and later that day I had a notification that he was doing a Facebook Live video. I decided to check it out. In the video I watched a pair of feet walk up to another pair of feet and Mr. Cubs asked if he could pray for the other person. The guy didn't really have a request, so Mr. Cubs prayed a general prayer, blessed the guy, and walked away.

I was shocked! This was the guy who didn't want to be saved, because he wanted to be selfish? My mind couldn't understand what was happening.

Then the next day, I got a Facebook Messenger call. Mr. Cubs was on the other side. I didn't really have time to answer it because I was trying to get some stuff done around the house, but I was so intrigued by the video that I really wanted to know what he was up to that day.

"Hey…uh…so… I went to Dunkin' Donuts, and I asked the lady behind the cash register if I could pray for her. And…she said no… So I asked the other girl working and she said she doesn't need prayer because she has the Holy Spirit. What is the Holy Spirit?" asked Mr. Cubs.

"Well, do you still have that little blue Bible we gave you?" I asked.

"Yeah," he responded.

"Well, you go get yours and I'll get mine and let me know when you're ready."

I had him open to the book of Acts and we walked through a few key passages that refer to the Holy Spirit. I also showed him the orange tab and explained that you get the Holy Spirit when you put Jesus in charge of your life. I told him that I didn't really know why that lady thought she didn't need prayer, because I have the Holy Spirit and I need a ton of prayer! I asked how he responded to them, and he said he'd just said, "Okay," and then left them alone. I thought maybe he'd want to talk more, but he hung up on me.

Every day from that point on, I checked his profile to see what he was posting. Every Sunday he would Facebook Live the church service that he was attending (which was in Spanish…and he doesn't speak Spanish). I decided to go back through his feed and check out his posts from before we met him. I realized this Mr. Cubs was no longer the man I had met that day at Dunkin' Donuts. That man was angry, obnoxious, and selfish. This new man was kind, prayed for people, and went to church.

I noticed that the movies he posted about were filthy before we met him, and everything he shared after was spiritual. All the music he'd talk about before was filled with vulgarity, and yet now he was listening to Christian rock bands. Even the content of his Facebook Live videos showed a difference. He would be at a Cubs game or a bar with a beer in his hands, getting plastered and hitting on the ladies, and now he was still posting about the Cubs (of course), but without the beer and the flirting. I was blown away. Scott and I would talk about it as we traveled to other cities, about how crazy transformed he was.

After a while I finally messaged Mr. Die-Hard Cubs Fan and said, "Hey, man. I know you said you didn't want to get saved and whatnot, but I want you to know I have seen a crazy difference in you. I have been watching you, and man, the Lord is moving in your life. The videos you watch aren't the same, the music you listen to isn't the same, and you're going to church faithfully. Are you sure you don't want to be all in? You're already living like it."

"Nah man. I just want to live my life and be free to be me. I just want to be selfish," he replied.

I share this story with nothing but respect and love for this guy. I watched his life transform while he didn't even know it was happening. I am believing for his salvation. One day, I will be able to rejoice with the angels when his name is written in the Lamb's Book of Life.

In Luke 15, Jesus tells three stories that have radically changed my life. Some tax collectors and "notorious sinners" (v.1) come to Jesus to hear him, but the religious leaders complained about it.

> So Jesus told them this story: "If a man has a hundred sheep and one of them gets lost, what will he do? Won't he leave the ninety-nine others in the wilderness and go to search for the one that is lost until he finds it? And when he has found it, he will joyfully carry it home on his shoulders. When he arrives, he will call together his friends and neighbors, saying, 'Rejoice with me because I have found my lost sheep.' In the same way, there is more joy in heaven over one lost sinner who repents and returns to God than over ninety-nine others who are righteous and haven't strayed away!
> Or suppose a woman has ten silver coins and loses one. Won't she light a lamp and sweep the entire house and search carefully until she finds it? And when she finds it, she will call in her friends and neighbors and say, 'Rejoice with me because I have found my lost coin.' In the same way, there is joy in the presence of God's angels when even one sinner repents. (Luke 15:1-10)

The last parable is a little longer, and is about a man with two sons. The younger son comes to his father and asks for his inheritance, and then after he receives it, blows it all. This son is now broke, starving, and working a job that doesn't provide for him. Finally he decides to return home and beg to be his father's servant because there, even the servants ate well.

> So he returned home to his father. And while he was still a long way off, his father saw him coming. Filled with love and compassion, he ran to his son, embraced him, and kissed him. His son said to him, "Father, I have sinned against both heaven and you, and I am no longer worthy of being called your son."
> But his father said to the servants… "We must celebrate with a feast, for this son of mine was dead and has now returned to life. He was lost, but now he is found." So the party began. (Luke 15:20-24)

There are some things that I really want to point out about this chapter. The first is this: Jesus is eating with and spending time with notorious sinners. They weren't just sinners but they were "notorious," which means they were extra sinful. The religious experts of the day were incredibly offended that He would spend so much time with these hooligans. This makes me think that Jesus thought it important not to just surround himself with other people who loved God, but those whose lives were a mess. The people Jesus spent His time with were disliked and some considered traitors, and here was Jesus dining with them. Who you spend your time with will show your priorities. If Jesus loved to dine with sinners, I want to dine with sinners.

Next I want to point out that the reason Jesus tells those parables is to respond to the religious fault-finders who are trying to tear Him down. He isn't saying this in response to what His disciples or the sinners that are with Him are saying, He's sort of defending them and giving them the right to be with Him. On top of that, He's informing the Pharisees that their priorities are off. They have missed the point. I don't think Jesus wanted to shame them as much as convict them to repent. With that in mind, let's dive into the third thing.

In each story or parable, Jesus uses the word "rejoice" or "celebrate." To me this is actually the point of telling the story. They are not just celebrating for the sake of it, but because the lost has been found, a son has come home, a sinner has repented. In my line of work these passages are quoted often. Usually you will hear someone sharing a testimony encouraging us to celebrate with the angels that are rejoicing because of the repentant sinner. One day while I was shouting for joy because someone gave their life to Jesus, something inside compelled me to look at this passage again. I believe it was the Holy Spirit. (FYI: I double-checked what I am about to say with multiple English translations and they all say pretty much the exact same thing.)

These three parables are told back to back. In verses 6 and 9 Jesus says the same thing. "Rejoice with me, because I have found…" Then in verse 23 when the prodigal son returns, Jesus says the dad calls for a celebration. What was lost has been found, sinners have repented, and that is cause for a party.

Verse 7 says that "there is more joy in heaven," verse 10 says "there is joy in the presence of God's angels," and verse 27 says "we are celebrating." For the longest time I had this mental picture of the angels taking a time out to cheer and shout and dance because a sinner repented, but as I looked at this passage again, I saw that it is not only the angels that are rejoicing. One verse says ALL of heaven, and the other says "in the presence of God's angels." This leads me to believe that our Heavenly Father is rejoicing along with the angels.

In fact it says in verse 28 that when the other son returns from the field and refuses to join the party, the father came out and begged him to join. In my mind I can hear the father saying with a laugh and a smile, "Rejoice with me. That which was lost has been found! Rejoice, sing (there is music in the party for the lost son), and dance (there was also dancing) WITH ME."

All of heaven celebrates. There is joy in the "presence" of God's angels. Both God and the angels are singing, and dancing, and celebrating because what was dead is now alive!

One day, I believe that I will be able to see Mr. Cubs in heaven. I believe that it is only a matter of time until he surrenders to Christ. On that day, you better believe that you're going to find me singing, and dancing, and shouting, and crying because my friend who was lost has been found. I can't wait to join the party in heaven rejoicing in the magnificence of our God who would send His Holy Spirit to take the time to go after that which was lost.

Today as we go out, as we intentionally share the gospel, let's keep our heavenly Father in mind. Let's make Him sing some more. Let's make Him dance some more. Let's fill heaven with the joy of a Father whose lost child has been found!

P.S. It is my hope and prayer that this book will help you to be confident enough in the Lord that you could implement what we have talked about into your daily routine. There is a really good chance you won't be a natural right away. Your heart may not burn right away. It will come. Schedule a time to share the gospel and stick to it. Don't think it will just happen on its own. One day it will, but right now you have to train yourself to share your faith.

Use this as a resource, but only alongside the Bible. When you run into a situation that you weren't ready for, dive into the scriptures, seek the Lord's face, and see what He says about the situation. Don't quit. It may be a lonesome journey. The path of lifestyle evangelism is not walked by the crowds right now, so be prepared. Try to find someone to run with if you can. It is always best to go in twos.

If you have any responses, testimonies, or stories you'd like to share, please send them to me!

If you read this book and you've never accepted the free gift of eternal life and you'd like to talk to someone about it, please feel free to contact me. I would love to answer any questions you have.

thefirewithinbook@gmail.com

To be Continued...

ACKNOWLEDGEMENTS

Obviously, I would like to thank Jesus, because without Him there is no book. Without Jesus, there are no stories to tell.

I would like to thank this massive group of people that have sacrificed their time and energy to make this possible, our donors and prayer partners. Without your generosity and your prayers I would not be able to do what I do the way I do it. Thank you.

Kyle And Laura Martin: Thank you for paving the way for guys like me to follow in your footsteps. Thank you for making the hard decisions and walking by faith even when it doesn't make sense. Thank you for coming to Indiana and wrecking my life (in a good way). Thank you for pouring yourself out over and over again to cities and our team. It is a honor to work with and for you.

Buzz Leonard: Thank you for molding my young brain. Many times when I wanted to quit or give up, you were there demanding more of me. Thank you for challenging my faith and my motives, my identity, and helping me to be rooted in Christ instead of my position.

Lela and Hiram Payne: You guys are amazing. Thank you for the prayers and the long conversations in cars when I am driving for hours at a time. Thank you for putting up with my ceaseless shenanigans and encouraging me to live a life of faith.

Gary Bohn: Your persistence and passion, unwavering even when the circumstances are difficult, have greatly influenced me. Thank you for your patience and willingness to put up with me. In many ways, most of my approach on the street comes from you. Thank you for teaching me what it looks like to love well. Also, thank you for the M&M's and hot tub time.

My team at Time to Revive: You guys put up with me and challenge me all the time to be the man God called me to be. Thank you for the late nights and early mornings and for putting up with my awful humor. Thank you for the hard conversations and the endless love. I love you guys.

My family: My wife who puts up with my escapades, horribly timed jokes, and inability to be organized. My son Josiah who has come with me on many of the adventures that are in this book, and for not being bitter because you have to be homeschooled. To the rest of my kids, Gideon, Mercy, and Anna, thanks for putting up with me. You're all still tiny, so you don't really have a choice, but one day you will, so I am thanking you in advance. Thank you for coming with me from city to city, and for praying for me when I'm on the street or training people. Thank you for being excited to see me. Thank you for fighting in the car to teach me how to be a good parent.

My dad: Thank you for teaching and showing me the importance of the Word of God. Thank you for teaching me how to work hard and to sing to the Lord while you're in tough situations and for supporting me in the seasons where I was an idiot…(insert dad joke).

My mom: I know you are my biggest supporter. Thank you for being excited to hear the stories, and for watching our kids so that Elly and I can breathe. Thank you for allowing us to raid your house…pretty much always. Thank you for loving my kids. Thank you for showing me as a child what it means to pray, when times are tough and when they're not.

My siblings: Thanks for randomly singing musicals at the top of your lungs and for supporting my family as we travel.

NEBTHOS: Thank you for taking a chance by publishing this.

Bea Wright and Dan Schuler: for the hard work you did editing my awful grammar and encouraging me as a writer and storyteller.

Jo Gilbert: for your sweet artwork on the cover.

Finally, I would like to thank YOU for being brave enough to read this.

ABOUT THE AUTHOR

The average person is confused by Jesse the Mexican Superhero. He dresses in mostly black, wears chains, and has an accent that no one can pinpoint. This gives him unique opportunities to share the gospel in unlikely areas to diverse people. He's a faithful husband, father, and servant of Jesus Christ. He likes John Wayne, Nacho Libre, Five Iron Frenzy, Mexican food, and laughing really loudly—especially with his family. He lives with his wife and kids in Milford, Indiana.

This is his first book.

To find a way to get involved with Time to Revive:
https://www.timetorevive.com/

For more information on Jesse Eisenhour or if you'd like to
begin supporting his family in ministry:
https://www.timetorevive.com/team-members/28

If you decided after reading this that you don't really like Jesse,
but you want to support a different team member, there are plenty
of great men and women that are helping to spread the good news.
https://www.timetorevive.com/team-members

TIME TO REVIVE CHEAT SHEET

*All of the following scriptures are in NASB

1. Yellow
   "For all have sinned and fall short of the Glory of God." (Rom. 3:23)
   Focus: sin

2. Black
   "For the wages of sin is death, but the free gift of God is eternal life in Christ Jesus our Lord." (Rom. 6:23)
   Focus: wages

3. Red
   "But God demonstrates His own love toward us, in that while we were yet sinners, Christ died for us." (Rom. 5:8)
   Focus: demonstrate

4. Blue
   "For by grace you have been saved through faith; and that not of yourselves, it is the gift of God; not as a result of works, so that no one may boast." (Eph. 2:8-9)
   Focus: works

5. Green
   "If you confess with your mouth Jesus as Lord, and believe in your heart that God raised Him from the dead, you will be saved; for with the heart a person believes, resulting in righteousness, and with the mouth he confesses, resulting in salvation." (Rom. 10:9-10)
   Focus: confess, Lord

6. Orange (Bonus Fry)
   Focus: discipleship, baptism, reading the Bible, praying, and sharing your faith

Back cover:
   "Is there anything or anyone that would keep you from accepting the free gift of life in Jesus today?"

   "Lord, I know I'm a sinner, but I thank You for Your Son, Jesus, who died on the cross for my sin and rose on the third day so that my sins could be forgiven and I can be with You and give my life to You. Please help me along the way and allow me to know You better each day. In Jesus' name I pray. Amen."

More Books Published by

www.nebthos.com

"Sound in the Gospel: for the knucklehead tech in all of us"
www.soundinthegospel.com

Coming Soon!

"Gaming in the Gospel: when just one more turn isn't enough"
www.gaminginthegospel.com